A
Growing-Up
Guide

To Haley
...tmas 2004
♥ you.
#2

Books by
Sandra Byrd
FROM BETHANY HOUSE PUBLISHERS

A Growing-Up Guide

Guide

What Girls Like <u>YOU</u> Want to Know

Sandra Byrd

BETHANYHOUSE
MINNEAPOLIS, MN 55438

Published by Bethany House Publishers
11400 Hampshire Avenue South
Bloomington, Minnesota 55438
www.bethanyhouse.com

Bethany House Publishers is a Division of
Baker Book House Company, Grand Rapids, Michigan.

Printed in the United States of America

Library of Congress Cataloging-in-Publication Data

Byrd, Sandra.
   A growing-up guide : what girls like you want to know / by Sandra Byrd.
     v.   cm.
Contents: My body —My feelings, moods, and emotions —Myself, my family, my friends —My life with God —School and activities.
   ISBN 0-7642-2752-1 (pbk.)
   1. Girls—Religious life—Juvenile literature. 2. Girls—Conduct of life—Juvenile literature. 3. Christian life—Biblical teaching—Juvenile literature. [1. Puberty. 2. Teenage girls. 3. Christian life.] I. Title.
   BV4551.3.B973   2003
   248.8'33—dc21   2003002035

For Elizabeth Byrd
I could have no greater joy than to hear
that my children live in the truth.

3 John 1:4

Contents

SANDRA BYRD lives near beautiful Seattle, between snow-capped Mount Rainier and the Space Needle, with her husband and two children (and let's not forget her golden retriever, Duchess). When she's not writing, she's usually reading, but she also likes to scrapbook, listen to music, and spend time with friends. Besides writing *A Growing-Up Guide*, she's also the author of the HIDDEN DIARY books and the bestselling SECRET SISTERS.

❀   ❀   ❀

You're not a little girl anymore.

Your legs are longer and your arms are stronger. Amazingly, you can read more difficult books and wrestle with tougher math problems. You're reaching a new level in your relationship with God—understanding more, and maybe asking more questions, too. You're learning to balance more than one friendship; some of your friends are boys.

From before we are born we are female, and yet we don't remain girls. We become young women and then women. It's an exciting time—and a little scary. The more you know, the less fear you'll have and the more you can take pleasure in the journey.

Young women have more opportunities than girls do—more to understand, more to consider, and more to manage. As you enjoy this book—by yourself or with your mom and dad or another trusted adult—I hope you learn more about yourself and others and see the opportunities ahead of you. Your future awaits. Step toward it with faith and excitement.

"I say this because I know what I have planned for you," says the Lord. "I have good plans for you. I don't plan to hurt you. I plan to give you hope and a good future."
JEREMIAH 29:11 ICB

[Caddie's father told her . . .] "A woman's work is something fine and noble to grow up to. . . . I want you to be a woman with a wise and understanding heart, healthy in body and honest in mind. Do you think you would like to be growing up into that woman now?"

. . . Something strange happened to Caddie in the night. When she awoke, she knew that she need not be afraid of growing up. It was not just sewing and weaving and wearing stays. It was something more thrilling than that. It was a responsibility, but, as Father spoke of it, it was a beautiful and precious one, and Caddie was ready to go and meet it.

from *Caddie Woodlawn*
by Carol Ryrie Brink

My Body

Growing up means . . .
I'm changing from a girl into a young woman!

Girls like you say . . .

"I'm glad I have a mom who is willing to listen and talk to me about the questions I have as I grow up."

"When I think about growing up I am very excited. It's going to be fun when I learn to drive."

"The best thing about getting as tall as my mom is that I get to wear her clothes."

"When I think about growing up . . . I get excited and scared at the same time!"

❀ ❀ ❀

Growing means changing. No matter how you grow—in your body, your mind, your relationships, or your spirit—it brings change. Sometimes change is easy, and sometimes it's hard. Sometimes we don't notice that we're changing, and other times we wonder if *everyone* notices, even if we don't want them to!

Change feels weird and a little scary because we're leaving something we know for something we don't know. Change also feels exciting because it brings new opportunities and adventures.

Have you ever seen one of those time-lapse movies where they start with a seed, and then it quickly becomes a little shoot, then a bigger plant, then a flower bud, then the full-blown blossom? Even though those changes happened over a long period of time, the film was sped up for viewing. When you watch it happen on screen, the whole process seems to zoom by in a minute. When you enter puberty, it can seem like a lot of changes are happening fast, too. But just like the flower seed, changes have been transforming your body for a long time. You just haven't seen them till now.

These changes are no surprise to God. He made your body to function just right, changing at the right times. He planned and prepared for you—and still does. As changes come, you can rest knowing that they are normal, natural, and intended just as God meant for them to be.

> *You made all the delicate, inner parts of my body and knit them together in my mother's womb. Thank you for making me so wonderfully complex! . . . Your workmanship is marvelous—and how well I know it. You were there while I was being formed in utter seclusion!*
>
> PSALM 139:13–15 TLB

You Asked

What IS puberty?

Puberty is the time in your life when your body is changing from that of a kid to that of an adult. It doesn't mean you are an adult yet, but it means that you are becoming one. You are becoming physically mature—that is, your body is making the change from girl to woman. This change doesn't happen overnight, even though it might seem like it. It all starts with hormones.

Yeah, what are hormones, anyway?

Your brain knows when it's time for you to begin growing up. It makes and sends hormones into your blood, which carries them throughout your body. Imagine it working like electricity.

Your body is like a lovely house with many levels and rooms. When the house is built, all of the rooms are wired for electricity, even though it might not be switched on in every room right away. When you're a child, the electricity is switched on in some rooms but not in all. As you near puberty, your brain and pituitary gland send signals to your body that it's time to mature. One by one, these hormones turn on different switches in your body. Each switch sends a signal to a different room in the house—a different part of your body. Your ovaries begin to get a little bigger inside you, for example. Growth hormones tell feet and legs and arms to grow longer.

Next, your body works with your adrenal gland. At puberty it produces the hormone androgen, which causes oily skin. It also causes fine hair to begin growing in your armpits and over the skin that covers your vaginal area. You'll get more hair on your legs. All of this hair will get thicker and coarser as you grow older. Your body also instructs the ovaries, which store the eggs to make babies, to produce more of a hormone called estrogen, which will lead to your developing breast buds and beginning menstruation. Your voice begins to become more mature.

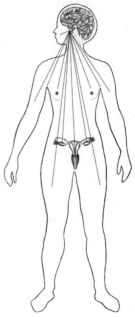

Some people's switches flip on in a different order. You might get a little hair on your vaginal area before you get breast buds. Or the other way around. That's okay. When all of the rooms are lit and all of your growth is complete, you'll have made the change from girl to young woman.

Try It!

Go through your house and turn off all of the lights. Then go from room to room and switch them on, one by one. Isn't it bright and fresh to see all of the lights on in every area, illuminating the special purpose and beauty of each room? What happens when all of the electricity is flowing freely throughout the house? How will it feel when your body is fully grown?

Can I control those hormones and all this other growth stuff?

Your body controls the release of hormones, just as it controls your beating heart, your breathing lungs, and your cleansing kidneys. God made these hormones turn on and off at just the right times for you. Sometimes we wish it would hurry up—it's fun to get older! Sometimes we wish those hormones would go away and we wouldn't have to grow up yet. These aren't choices we can make, though. There is a time to be a girl and there is a time to become a young woman. There is a right and proper season for each of these.

> *There is a time for everything, and a season for every activity under heaven.*
> ECCLESIASTES 3:1 NIV

You can keep track of the changes, though. Watching the normal progress your body makes at a steady pace will make you feel better. Put a check mark by each of the following changes you've noticed about yourself.

Wonderfully Made
Changes I've Noticed

- ☒ growing taller
- ☒ changing voice—more womanish, less little-girlish
- ☒ bigger feet and hands
- ☐ oilier skin

- [ ] blackheads
- [ ] pimples
- [x] fine hairs in my armpits
- [x] hair in my pubic area (near vagina)
- [ ] body odor
- [x] hairy legs
- [x] breasts beginning to grow
- [x] waist getting narrow
- [x] hips getting a little curvier
- [ ] discharge on my underwear
- [x] menstruation starting
- [x] menstruation becoming regular
- [x] not growing taller as fast anymore

Does puberty ever stop?

Yes. Different bodies begin to turn these switches on at different times and at different rates. Normal puberty can take between two and six years from start to finish, depending on the girl. Puberty doesn't start in a hurry or stop in a hurry. Rather, it builds up slowly and then tapers off slowly, too. Because these things happen to different girls at different times, it's important to know that you may get your period well before, or well after, many of your closest friends. It's all normal, though. Each body has its own perfect rhythm.

When puberty is complete, you will be physically mature. You'll be as tall as you'll ever be—most girls grow only one or two more inches after they begin to menstruate. Because many girls reach puberty before most boys do, you'll probably be taller than a lot of boys—but only temporarily. They'll catch up soon. Boys go through puberty, too—although their hormones work differently because they are developing the body of a man. Boys change both physically and emotionally, too, just like girls do. Sometimes we think they have it easier, but they really don't. Their changes are just different from ours.

After puberty, your body will still produce the hormones that flow throughout your body; they'll just be regulating it as the body of a grown young woman now.

Speaking of the body of a young woman, I think my breasts are growing.

As you become a young woman, you will begin to develop the breasts of a woman. As a girl, your breasts were flat skin, with only a small portion, the nipple, raised. As you begin puberty, you will develop breast buds first.

Breast buds are when your breasts first begin to swell from the chest. Usually you feel a hard little lump when you touch there—that's the breast tissue and milk ducts under your skin developing. Your breasts will continue to swell, with the nipple areas being large at first. As you mature, your breasts will continue to grow for several years. Your milk ducts won't become active until you are pregnant.

Why are some people's breasts bigger than others? Will my breasts grow big?

Genetics, meaning the biology you inherited from your mom and your dad when you were made, will determine how large your breasts will be. If your mom has large breasts, you may, too. If hers are small, yours may also be. The size of your body matters, too. If you're a smaller girl, your breasts may be smaller; heavier girls may have heavier breasts. There is no potion or vitamin or exercise that will make your breasts bigger or smaller than their natural size in a healthy body.

Looking Forward: Buying a Bra

When your breasts begin to grow, you'll need to begin looking at appropriate undergarments. Your breast tissue needs support, and you'll want to be modest. Modesty means you don't allow your breasts to show through your clothing. At first, you can probably wear a camisole or a sports bra and that will be enough. When your breasts begin to get a little larger, though, you'll need to find a properly fitting bra.

Sometimes moms and daughters like to make a big deal out of buying a first bra—a special trip to a department store, followed by lunch. Sometimes they just like to make it a part of their everyday shopping. You choose what's best for you!

Pop Quiz
What Size Bra Do You Need?

Ask your mom to measure you for a bra. Here's what you'll need to do.

Bra Size Have your mom measure around your rib cage—just below your breasts—with a tape measure. Make sure the tape measure is firmly against your skin but not pulling at all. Bra sizes come in even numbers. If your rib cage measurement is an odd number, say 27 inches, add 5 to it to come up with a bra size of 32. If your measurement is even, say 30 inches, add 4 to it, which would make a bra size of 34.

Your rib cage measurement: _____

Your bra size: _____

Cup Size Have your mom take the tape measure and measure all the way around again, this time crossing over the fullest part of your breasts. Take your rib cage measurement (above) and subtract it from the number you just got, in inches, by measuring across your breasts. How many inches is the difference?

    AA cup: up to ½-inch difference
    A cup: ½- to 1-inch difference
    B cup: 1- to 2-inch difference
    C cup: 2- to 3-inch difference

Your cup size: _____

So if your first measurement was 28 inches and your second measurement was 29 inches, you would wear a bra size 32A. If your first measurement was 27 inches and your second measurement was 27 inches, you would wear a bra size 32AA.

You'll want to remeasure every six months or so. As you grow, your breasts will grow, too. A bra that is too tight will pinch and ride up on your chest. If a bra is too big and doesn't fit snugly, it will twist around and the cups will cave in.

Trying on Bras

Now that you know your bra size, you need to try the bras on. If you are buying a bra that has hook-and-eye closures, make sure you buy one that you can comfortably hook in the loosest eye(s). As the bra is laundered, it will stretch some, and you'll want to be able to move to the tighter fit. You'll also want to make sure the straps across your shoulders don't pinch and that the straps aren't so close to the neck (like some sports bras are) that you'll be able to see the straps underneath T-shirts with wide necks. If your measurements were close to the next category and that size fits you better, go ahead and buy the one that fits the best.

Will everyone know I have a bra on?

It can be strange at first to wear a bra. You might wonder if anyone can notice. Some people may, but remember, the rest of the world is used to knowing that women wear bras. If you have a well-fitting bra and modest clothes on, no one should be able to notice anything out of the ordinary. If you ever find your bra strap is showing, don't panic. Just casually slip your finger up to it and slide it back under your shirt. The less fuss you make about it, the less attention anyone else will pay to it.

Bras aren't like underpants. They don't need to be changed every day, or washed each time you wear them, unless it's a sports bra or you've been sweaty. Washing your bras every two or three wears is a good system. That way you won't have to buy too many bras at one time, because you'll probably be changing sizes fairly regularly till you're sixteen or seventeen years old.

Looking Forward: Getting Your Period

Each girl and woman has two ovaries, two fallopian tubes, and a uterus. These are inside you, located below your belly button. When you grow up, get married, and want children, these organs will help you to have them. An egg will travel down one of the fallopian tubes. When it becomes a baby, it will rest inside your uterus and grow till it's ready to be born.

During and after puberty, your body begins to prepare for this possibility each month. Even though you are not ready to have a baby and won't have a baby for many years, this cycle begins now and will keep happening each month for years after you're finished having babies or even if you never have children. It's the natural rhythm of a woman's body. From puberty onward, your body will send an egg down one of those tubes each month. Because you're not going to have a baby yet, it doesn't get made into a baby, and it doesn't need someplace to rest and grow. Your body knows this. It causes the soft lining of your uterus to shed, along with fluids and the unused egg. All of this flows out of your body through your vagina. When that is shed, we call it menstruation, or getting your period.

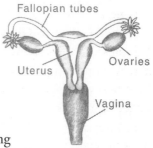

Fallopian tubes

Ovaries

Uterus

Vagina

You Asked

Is it really blood? Does it hurt?

Some blood does come out, because there is blood in the uterine lining. The lining also comes out, which sometimes looks like lumps or clots. It's all healthy, though. It's your body's way of taking care of itself, as it was meant to do.

Sometimes you will get cramps just before or at the beginning of your period. It might feel like a squeezing in your lower tummy area, on one or both sides, or an ache and squeezing in the center, right above your pubic bone. It might feel like a strong backache. Yours may feel different from any of your friends'. Some girls don't feel cramps, some feel them a little, and some feel them a lot. Your mom can give you a hot water bottle or hot gel pack to sleep with if that helps, or she can give you some ibuprofen. Sometimes cramps can make you feel a little sick to your stomach. It can help to drink some ginger ale. The cramps won't last your entire period. And it doesn't hurt at all when the menstrual fluids actually come out of your body.

Why is it called a period?

When someone uses the word *period,* they often mean a section in time. Someone can refer to the Elizabethan period, which means history around the time that Elizabeth I was queen of England. A second-period class means the second section of time during the school day. Our menstrual periods happen regularly, almost the same time every month, once we have had them for a little while. It's a period of time.

We menstruate in a cyclical pattern—it happens in cycles. When you think about it, there are a lot of cyclical patterns in your life. Seasons are cyclical—winter, spring, summer, fall, then winter again. Our days are cyclical—they begin in the morning, go through till night, and start all over again. The sun rises and sets as God arranged for it to do. The moon has regular, exact cycles—new moon, half moon, full moon, half moon, and new moon again. It's comforting to recognize patterns, because it helps us know what to expect. In spring we expect rain, and in summer we expect to have school vacation, so we know what to plan for.

The same is true with your period. It happens cyclically— regularly. Once you start having your periods, you can begin to track what to expect. Periods come, on average, every twenty-five to thirty-two days. Many women and girls, but not all, have their periods every four weeks, or every twenty-eight days. God created your body wonderfully well, as He created every other thing to work according to His plan. Relax, knowing that He created your body to work exactly as it should.

You made the moon to mark the seasons, and the sun always knows when to set.

PSALM 104:19 NCV

You created me.

PSALM 119:73B

How can I track my periods? How will it help?

You've probably already got a calendar in your room to help you keep track of important events. Maybe you mark down sleepovers or plans with friends or when you'll have a test. Once you get your period, you can begin to mark that down, too.

When you first get your period, write a small letter *P* on the corner of the date on which it happened. Day One of your period is always the day you first spot any blood on your underwear or on the toilet paper when you wipe. Make a small

X on the calendar for each day that you menstruate after Day One. Write an *E* on your calendar to show when your period ends. You can also track other changes on your calendar, such as changes associated with PMS. It may take a couple of years before your periods become regular, and that's normal. It is still helpful to keep track.

What is PMS?

PMS stands for premenstrual syndrome. It refers to the things happening in your body just before you menstruate. Some women have several PMS symptoms, while others have very few or none at all. Over the years you will come to recognize and manage your body's unique cycles.

Some women have physical changes just before their periods. They might have tender breasts, cramps, or headaches. The same hormones that cause our bodies to begin to menstruate can also cause emotional changes just before we menstruate each month. Some girls feel very sad or easily angered, or they may lack motivation. These changes are all temporary and will go away shortly after your period actually begins. There's more to read about the emotional changes in the next section of this book.

Tracking these things on your calendar can help. Write words like *cramps, headache, crabby, easily angered,* or *sad* on days that you feel that way—even if you're not menstruating yet. Learning that you always get a headache the day before your period or that you feel sad and crabby for two days before your period and then recognizing that it goes away after you begin to bleed helps you to feel more secure and in control because you know what to expect and when. Sometimes these emotional changes begin to happen months or even years before you actually menstruate, and they can even happen cyclically. It will help you feel better to see that there's a pattern, that you can handle it, and that the changes are temporary and short-lived.

My Calendar

January 2004

S	M	T	W	T	F	S
				1	2	3
4	5	6	7	8	9 *Sleepover!*	10 *ZZZ* ☹
11	12	13	14 *PMS*	15 *PMS*	16	17
18 ☹	19 *P*	20 *X*	21 *X*	22 *E*	23	24
25	26	27	28	29	30 *Math test - STUDY!!!*	31

ZZZ = angry   ☹ *= sad*   *P = period starts*   *E = period ends*

How will I know when I'm getting my period for the first time? How should I take care of myself?

Getting your period won't be a total surprise, because you'll be noticing some other changes, like the checklist you did a few pages ago. You'll see your body changing, and you'll be prepared.

Go shopping with your mom and get a small zippered bag that will hold feminine protection products—things like pads, liners, and tampons, which trap the flow and keep it secure during the days you get your period. You will probably have a light flow that lasts only a short time at first, so you'll need light protection to start with. Your mom can show you how each of these products works, and together you can decide which is right for you. None of the products hurt when they are used correctly. If you begin using one and it hurts or doesn't contain the flow well, ask your mom to help you figure it out.

Don't be embarrassed. Your mom has used these products for a long time, and she's there to help. Better to ask a quick question now and feel comfortable and secure than to skip asking and wonder if something will go wrong.

Just before your period, you might get a few cramps. Some girls notice discharge a few days before their periods. Discharge is a sticky substance, kind of like drying glue, that comes from your vagina. It's nothing bad—in fact, it's a way your body cleans itself. As long as it's clear, whitish, or slightly yellow, don't worry about it.

Most girls don't know exactly when their period will come. Remember, though, it's a light flow at first, more like little spots. You'll probably just notice it on the toilet paper or as a small stain on your underpants. If you don't have protection products with you, you can roll a small amount of toilet paper and line your underpants with that till you can get home and get to the products you and your mom set aside. Don't panic—it'll be okay. From then on you should carry your zippered bag in your purse or backpack just to be prepared. Nobody will know.

Ask Your Mom

. . . to help you prepare a kit for your period. Ask her when she first got her period and what her experience was.

Other Changes
As your body matures, it will make other changes, too.

Will I get acne?

One of the switches that gets turned on during puberty is the one that causes your skin's oil glands to begin producing more oil. These glands are usually on your face and your back, although some girls get pimples on their upper chest or neck, too. When you combine this extra oil with dead skin cells, dirt, and bacteria, you get pimples and blackheads developing in the skin's pores.

Some people are more likely, genetically, to develop acne, which is a stronger case of pimples and blackheads covering more area of the skin. Other people don't have many zits at all. If you wash your face carefully morning and night and use products to clean the pores, like Stridex cloths, you'll be keeping those pores from clogging as much as you possibly can. You can also use benzoyl peroxide on your skin—both face and back—dabbing it on any pimples to help them dry up and heal more quickly.

Keeping your hands and your hair off of your face will help, too. Your hands have natural oils on them, and whenever you touch your skin, you're transferring that oil. Same with your hair.

For some fun and interesting ways to care for your skin, you might enjoy reading *The Inside-Out Beauty Book*.

So my hair has more oil in it, too?

Yep. It's the same oil glands at work as the ones in your face. Make sure you keep your hair off of your face, because it can transfer oil to places where you don't need any more right now!

Face:

- Wash twice daily with mild soap and warm water. Don't scrub! Scrubbing makes the irritation worse.
- Use wipe-away pads containing salicylic acid once a day. If

you notice it's making your skin more irritated, stop.

- Use a product with benzoyl peroxide in it to help dry up and heal any blemishes and prevent future blackheads.

Back:

- Bathe or shower nearly every day.
- Wash your back with a loofah on a stick. Your back needs to be scrubbed lightly, and since you can't reach a washcloth back there, you'll need another tool.
- Use the same products that you use on your face, if needed. Get your mom to apply them for you.

Hair:

- Use a cleansing shampoo for oily hair.
- Wash your hair at least every other day—every day if it's especially oily—from now on.
- Apply conditioners sparingly from your ears down—don't use them on the crown of your head.

Anything else?

Yes. Because your oil and sweat glands are working overtime to get you through puberty, you will develop more body odor. Body odor forms when sweat and bacteria mingle with dust and skin cells on your body and in your clothing. It thrives in areas that are moist and warm—like your feet inside of your shoes and socks, your armpits, and near your vagina.

Because of this, you'll need to bathe more regularly. Personal hygiene means practicing cleanliness to encourage good health and well-being. You don't feel good—or smell good—without it.

Taking a shower every day is probably a good idea. If your hair isn't too greasy yet, you can wash it every other day and just wash your skin every day. If your hair *is* greasy, you can wash it every day, too.

When you wash your skin, you'll need to use a washcloth, not just your hand. A washcloth helps to remove the dead cells, keeping your skin fresh and healthy. Be sure to thoroughly clean under your arms and gently wash inside the folds of your vagina.

Do I need to wear deodorant?

You might. Deodorant is something that prevents or covers up odor. Antiperspirant prevents or dries out sweat so that it doesn't come through your clothing. Some products combine both antiperspirant and deodorant. There are products both for armpits and for feet. Talk with your mom if you feel you could use either of these.

I think I'm ready to shave. How do you know for sure if you are?

You and your mom can discuss when you are ready to shave your armpits or your legs. It's important to know that you don't have to shave them for health reasons. In many places in the world, women do not shave at all. In our culture we normally do. When you get to the point where you feel a bit embarrassed about the amount of hair on your legs or in your armpits, it's probably time to have that talk with your mom.

During puberty your hormones will make the hair in your armpits and on your legs (and even, for some girls, on your arms) thicker and darker. It will begin to grow faster.

Does it hurt to shave? Is it dangerous?

When you shave, you'll use a razor, which is a blade. You'll want to be careful. There are a number of razors that are designed to be used safely.

Many women like to shave at the end of a bath or a shower, because the hot water has softened the hair on their skin. Apply a shaving cream, and then carefully shave your legs, starting at the bottom and working toward the top of the leg. If you shave against the way the hair grows—from bottom to top—you're more likely to get all of the hair. This is true with your armpits, too.

You may need to shave your armpits or the lower part of your legs more often than the upper part of your legs. Shave slowly and keep a firm grip on the razor. Always throw the razor or the blade away as soon as it's dull. A dull razor is more likely to cut you.

If you do cut yourself, don't panic. Rinse the area well, and when you get out of the tub, apply some toilet paper till it stops bleeding. You can cover the cut with a bandage, and it will be okay soon.

This is embarrassing—but I'm getting some hair above my upper lip. Am I going to have a mustache?

All people have hair above their lips after puberty. Most women have very fine, light hair that is hard to see and easy to ignore. Some women have darker hair, and it's a bit thicker. That's normal, too. If it bothers you, ask your mom about a mild depilatory—a special cream that will gently smooth the hair away.

My gums bleed now when I brush my teeth. Is that because of puberty, too?

Maybe. Those same hormones that are helping you to grow are also sending more blood to the area around your teeth. The gums can sometimes become swollen, and that might make them more tender and likely to bleed.

If you've had braces put on or taken off recently, it can cause the same thing. Be sure to brush at least twice a day, floss at least once a day, and visit your dentist regularly. She can help you get your teeth ready for adulthood, too.

Now that I'm getting older, I should be able to stay up later. Right?

Your body is growing at an incredible rate right now. Some doctors feel that during puberty you may actually need *more* sleep than when you were a younger child because your body is doing so much work on the inside. When you get that sleep will depend on your family, your school and activities schedule, and your individual body's needs.

You need at least nine hours of sleep per night. If you don't get them, your body is going to let you know it's not happy. You'll be draggy, moody, and cranky. You'll be tired. It'll be hard to concentrate on your work or activities. Part of growing up is taking responsibility for yourself—for your sleep habits, your exercise habits, and your eating habits.

Speaking of eating, I think I'm fat.

Our society has a love-hate relationship with food and with our bodies, especially for girls. As Christians, we need to love our bodies—God created them especially for us and has chosen to live within them. We are also to enjoy the food He provides for us. Loving your body is a way to love yourself. Loving yourself is very important to your well-being—as a young woman now and through all the years as you grow up. Say it out loud: "I love myself. I'm a good person, inside and out." Come on, say it. Why is that so hard?

Each of us is given an individual body—no one else has exactly your body or genetic makeup. We have different lengths of legs, different muscle makeup. Some of us are small boned, some are large boned. Some of us are skinny no matter what—and we sometimes feel too skinny. Some of us are curvy no matter what, and we can feel fat. The first step to accepting yourself and avoiding a lifelong cycle of trying to be like others is to accept that we are all different, like many beautiful fish in a tropical sea. God made you that way, right?

How do I know if I'm at a healthy weight for my age or not?

If you're too thin, that may be unhealthy. You might not be eating enough to grow well. You may get tired or run-down before your friends do, or it might be hard to do your best schoolwork. On the other hand, you can also weigh too much, and that's unhealthy, too. It can be bad for your heart and can make it hard to keep up with sports or other activities. It can make sleeping or breathing more difficult. An important part of being healthy is keeping at a good weight for your height and build—not too thin, not too heavy.

One tool that doctors use is called a BMI chart. BMI stands for body mass index. It helps you to find a range of healthy weights for your size and age. You need to remember, though—no tool is perfect. It can't take into account if you have small or large bones or more muscle than other kids. More muscular kids are going to weigh more—and they may be perfectly healthy. Figure out your BMI, and then find it in the chart on the next page. If your measurement is lower than the fifth percentile or higher than the ninety-fifth percentile for your age, it might be good to talk to your doctor. No matter what your BMI is, your doctor can see your build and make a more accurate assessment. Ask her at your next visit if your body is at a healthy place.

Remember—your BMI is not going to be the same as anyone else's. You might be your most healthy at a 20 BMI while your best friend may be most healthy at a BMI of 18 or 22. That's why there's a range. For example, if you're ten years old, your BMI can be anywhere from 14 to 23 and still be in the target range. Different levels for different bodies. All healthy and all pretty.

Determine Your BMI

1. Weigh yourself, in pounds, and write it down. For example, 105 pounds.

2. Measure yourself, in inches, and multiply that number by itself to get the **height factor**. For example, if you're 60 inches tall, you'd multiply 60 times 60 to get 3,600.
3. Divide your weight by the height factor. For example, 105 divided by 3,600 equals .0292.
4. Multiply this number by 703. The total is your BMI. In our example, it would be 20.5, or rounded up to 21.

Match up your age and BMI to the chart on the next page. If you like, you can make a dot and go back and reassess this every year to see how you're growing. Don't do it more often than that, though. It's a tool to help you, not to obsess over.

Exercise

What is exercise? According to the dictionary, it's using something, bringing it into action. Sometimes we think we have to be running or lifting weights to exercise. There's nothing wrong with those kinds of things—in moderation. But most of us can get into action in other exciting ways. Exercise can be even more fun when you do it with others. Here are some ideas:

- walking around the block or walking outside at recess while chatting with friends
- biking around the neighborhood
- swimming with family or friends at a local pool
- playing tag, badminton, volleyball, tetherball, basketball
- walking the dog
- joining a sport
- taking a dance class or doing an exercise video

Because we live in a world where we sit a lot—in class, at home, in front of the computer or the television, or with a book—it's important to build exercise into your life. You have to do it on purpose, make a plan, and stick to it. Experts advise

BMI for Age

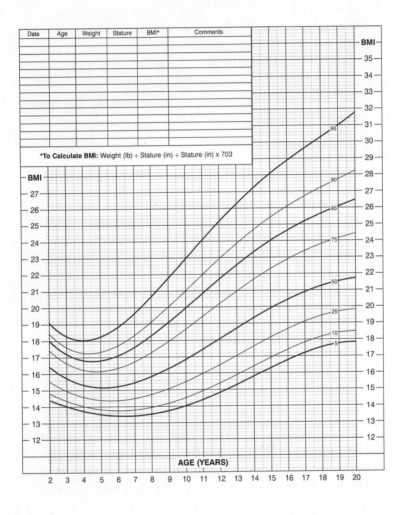

Date	Age	Weight	Stature	BMI*	Comments

*To Calculate BMI: Weight (lb) ÷ Stature (in) ÷ Stature (in) x 703

AGE (YEARS)

doing something active every day. If you're not active enough to build up a sweat several times a week, you need to add more activity.

Here are some of the benefits of regular exercise:

- Builds strong heart, muscles, and bones.
- Helps even out moods, including lowering stress and anxiety. A discouraged mood can often be lifted with exercise!
- Helps build endurance—good for sports, play, and all kinds of things.
- Circulates blood—good for skin, hair, nails, and all body organs.
- Helps you sleep better.
- Helps you concentrate on schoolwork better.
- Helps you live a longer and healthier life.
- Helps you maintain a healthy weight.
- Helps you enjoy life more. Kids active in sports or who exercise often have a better sense of well-being than those who don't.

Ask Your Mom

. . . to join an aerobic dance class with you once a week or to buy an exercise videotape the two of you can share.

Working toward being healthy and fit is a good way to take care of your body, which is a gift from God. It will also help you to be prepared for His service whenever God calls. What are your plans to get exercise into your life and keep it there?

1)

2)

3)

Food

If I want to eat healthy, does that mean I can never have another soda?

No. A Coke at the movies or cake at a party once in a while is a treat. It's drinking soda every day—and skipping water and milk, things your body really needs—that is the problem. Learn to save treats for special occasions. Most weeks should have no more than a couple of special occasions.

As you grow, you will become more and more in charge of your eating habits. Right now your parents are helping build these food habits. Later, your mom and dad won't be with you every minute to monitor how you're eating. At friends' houses and school and other places, you're probably already making some of your own choices. It's not easy, but you can do it.

The three main things to control are

- how often you eat
- how much you eat
- what you eat

How often should I eat?

Everyone needs to start the day out with breakfast. The best way for your body to handle food is to eat small or medium amounts of food several times a day—it's like giving it fuel to run on all day. Your body feels well taken care of. When you starve your body—go too long without food—you can get crabby and tired. You won't do your best work or always be able to stay awake.

If you eat too much at once, it's hard for your body to handle it all. You might get a sick stomach, heartburn, or really tired as your body tries to cope with digesting all of the food. Eating too much or too little can bring on mood swings, too. No kidding. No fun.

Eat three medium-sized meals a day, spaced about four hours apart. If your dinner will be more than four hours after lunch, eat a small, healthy snack in the afternoon. If you're eating all the time, you're getting too much food, and your body never gets to rest from digestion. Make sure your meals are balanced.

The key is to eat when you're truly hungry and stop when you're satisfied. Eat slowly so your body can send you the signals. Don't eat again till you start to feel physically hungry again. And don't wait past when your body says it's hungry to eat, either.

Although moms and dads help us to make wise choices, one day everything that goes into your mouth will be up to you. If you don't give yourself the right food to work, play, and grow, who will?

How much should I eat?

A good place to start is to read the labels on what you eat. They almost always say what a serving is. But don't be surprised at how small most serving sizes really are!

Investigate

- Measure out three-fourths of a cup of cereal and add one cup of low-fat milk. Is that what your bowl of cereal usually looks like? _____
- How many servings are in a typical bottle of sports drink? _____
- How many potato chips make a serving? _____
- Compare how many grams of sugar are in a serving of yogurt compared with a serving of soft drink. What did you find? _____
- Are you satisfied at half a hamburger? Why eat the rest, then? _____

The biggest struggle many of us have is portion control. If you stick with appropriate portions and the foods that the food pyramid suggests, that's a great place to start.

What is the food pyramid? Does it tell me what to eat?

The food pyramid was developed by doctors and scientists to help people understand what kinds of and how much food they need to eat. The pyramid is a guideline, not a strict rule. There are no "bad" foods. Just pay attention to eating healthily much of the time.

Here's what the pyramid looks like, with the suggested foods:

Food Guide Pyramid
A Guide to Daily Food Choices

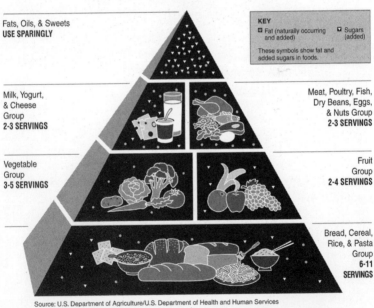

Fats, Oils, & Sweets
USE SPARINGLY

KEY
☐ Fat (naturally occurring and added) ☐ Sugars (added)
These symbols show fat and added sugars in foods.

Milk, Yogurt, & Cheese Group
2-3 SERVINGS

Meat, Poultry, Fish, Dry Beans, Eggs, & Nuts Group
2-3 SERVINGS

Vegetable Group
3-5 SERVINGS

Fruit Group
2-4 SERVINGS

Bread, Cereal, Rice, & Pasta Group
6-11 SERVINGS

Source: U.S. Department of Agriculture/U.S. Department of Health and Human Services

Here are the portion sizes that are best for you. Find your age, find what kind of food you're looking for, and determine portion size.

Number of Servings

Dairy	Meat	Fruits & Vegetables	Grains
Child: 2 to 3 servings Teen: 4 to 5 servings	Child & Teen: 2 to 3 servings	Child & Teen: 5 to 9 servings	Child & Teen: 6 to 11 servings

Serving Sizes

	Dairy	Meat	Fruits & Vegetables	Grains
6 to 9 years old	¾ to 1 cup	2 to 3 ounces	½ to 1 cup	1 to 2 slices or 1 cup
10 to 12 years old	1 cup	2 to 4 ounces	1 cup	2 slices or 1 cup
Teens	1 cup	3 to 4 ounces	1 cup	2 slices or 1 cup

Pop Quiz
How Many Servings Do You Need Each Day of the Following?

Dairy:
Meat:
Fruits and Vegetables:
Grains:

Try It!

Fill in the pyramid below for an entire day. See how your diet measures up. Remember, occasional treats in moderate amounts are okay, as long as they don't crowd out the more nutritious foods.

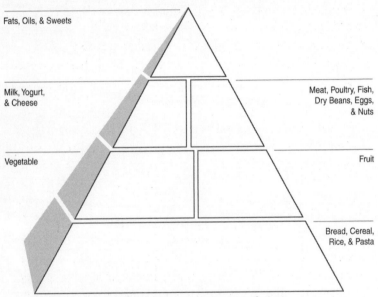

Fats, Oils, & Sweets

Milk, Yogurt, & Cheese

Meat, Poultry, Fish, Dry Beans, Eggs, & Nuts

Vegetable

Fruit

Bread, Cereal, Rice, & Pasta

Source: U.S. Department of Agriculture/U.S. Department of Health and Human Services

Half of my weight?

That's right. Much of your body weight is made up of water. Water is necessary to all living things—including you! Your body needs water to regulate temperature (so you don't overheat), to digest your food, to wash wastes out of your body, and to keep the organs inside—including your brain!—running smoothly.

On any given day your body uses up many cups of water just to keep it going. You need to replace that water. How?

- Drink more water. Make sure you drink several glasses of water each day.
- Don't drink caffeine. Not only will it make you hyper, and not only can you get addicted to it (it's a drug), but it makes you have to go to the bathroom more often. That wastes water your body can use.
- Eat fruits and vegetables and drink your milk.
- Don't drink sports drinks, teas, or other beverages with herbs like ginseng or guarana in them. These herbs can act like drugs. They can do bad things to your body and are not meant for children.

Don't forget—your body can go for several days without food if necessary but not without water. You need water every day in order to live.

Ask Your Mom

. . . if you can make a personalized water bottle. Get a plastic water bottle with a straw in it or with a resealable lid. You can personalize the bottle with puff paints, stickers, or colored permanent markers. Take it with you wherever you go—in the car, to school, and especially to sports. If you have refreshing water handy, there won't be the temptation to drink soda instead. Make one for a friend, brother, or sister, too!

Making Good Choices

Smoking Smoking rots your teeth, tongue, and gums, it makes your breath stink and your nails yellow, and it ruins your overall good health. Here are some questions kids might ask, with answers from the Surgeon General's Report on the Centers for Disease Control and Prevention's Web site:

Don't a lot of kids smoke?

Not really. "Only 13 percent of (or 13 out of 100) adolescents have smoked in the last 30 days. And only 8 percent are 'frequent' smokers. That means most kids—87 percent, to be exact—are smart enough not to smoke."

Smoking only affects the health of older people, right?

"You already know that smoking can cause things like cancer and heart disease, but the report also lists symptoms that start to develop as soon as you smoke your first cigarette—no matter how young you are. These include shortness of breath, coughing, nausea, dizziness, and 'phlegm production.'"

Will tobacco make me more likely to try other drugs?

"Many times tobacco is the first drug used by kids who use alcohol and illegal drugs. . . . Compared with nonsmokers, kids who smoke are 3 times more likely to use alcohol. They're 8 times more likely to smoke marijuana, and 22 times more likely to use cocaine. Scary, huh?"

If I try it, can't I just quit?

"Most teens who smoke want to stop. Nearly half of the high school seniors in the survey said they'd like to quit smoking. But they can't because . . . 'most young people who smoke daily are addicted to nicotine.'"

Did You Know?

"The typical smoker spends $700 a year on cigarettes!" With that money, you could

- support eighteen families in Ghana for one year through World Vision;

- take three friends to the movies—with popcorn, soda, and candy—every month and still have money left over for a pizza at home;
- buy 140 of your favorite paperback books or about 50 CDs.

Alcohol and Drugs Alcohol is a drug, and it is not legal for anyone under the age of twenty-one to drink it. Drunk driving is the number one killer of teenagers. People over twenty-one can drink alcohol in moderation if they choose to do so.

Nonprescription drugs are never legal. Using medicines that a doctor prescribed for someone else is never legal, either.

Alcohol and drugs enter the bloodstream and go throughout every system of your body. They affect your brain, your heart, your lungs, and your digestive system. They change the way you think. People under the influence of drugs or alcohol do not make wise decisions. They can't think clearly, see or hear clearly, or react quickly to dangerous situations. They are prone to accidents. Some drugs can make you addicted the first time you try them. Others just lead you away from the people, activities, and things you love.

Kids who drink or do drugs do not do well in school. They may even be expelled. Many people become addicted to smoking, alcohol, or drugs. This means they become slaves of that addiction.

You've heard it before. Just say no. Others say no, even if they say it quietly. You can, too.

You may say, "I am allowed to do anything." But I reply, "Not everything is good for you." And even though "I am allowed to do anything," I must not become a slave to anything.

1 CORINTHIANS 6:12

As we grow up, we are faced with changes and choices. Our bodies are changing according to the plan that was set in motion as we were made in our mothers' wombs. We have more and more choices—what to eat, what to drink, how to protect ourselves from dangerous substances.

You've heard the saying "Knowledge is power." It's true. Now you know what's happening to your body, so you can feel comfortable and confident. Excited! You'll be a young woman soon. Knowing what choices you have—and how to make good ones—will allow you to keep that beautiful, God-given body clean, safe, and healthy.

No matter what changes are going on—and your whole life will be a series of changes—one thing is true. God never changes. He is always faithful, always in control. Change leads us to new places, but the Bible promises that God will go before us, sticking with us all the time. Grab His hand and walk on!

The Lord himself will go before you. He will be with you; he will not leave you or forget you. Don't be afraid, and don't worry.

DEUTERONOMY 31:8 NCV

Poetry

I dream about growing up.
There are lots of things that will happen to me.
Changes.
New friends.
Different trends.
But right now, I like this age.
(That's all. Turn the page.)
   —by Tavia, age 11

I wonder why, it's so hard to know,
I wonder how the timeline go
I wonder how God made me so.
   It's so hard to know
How, What, Where, Why.
Will someone please tell me why?
I'm having trouble understanding so . . .
Tell me please!!!!
   —by Katherine, age 10

Mom and Me
Ideas From Girls Like You

"We had a pajama party—no dads or brothers allowed. We read a book together about growing up and the changes that happen, and we talked about what it was like for Mom. We had popcorn and watched a girl movie afterward. We talked about anything and asked questions, too. Questions are always important, anytime."

Debbie and Sarah, age 11

"My mom is sometimes brave enough to do up my hair in new ways, and I am brave enough to wear it in public."

Kaylynn and Emily, age 12

"Tori loves to shop but I absolutely don't like to, so she knows how special it is when I take her."

Bev and Tori, age 12

My Feelings, Moods, and Emotions

Growing up means . . . I'm becoming comfortable, confident, and self-controlled!

Girls like you say . . .

"People change as quickly and endlessly as the seasons or moods. But our God is timeless; you can always count on Him to love you and be there for you."

"We live with the three-day rule at our house. I heard this explanation once. For the disciples, things looked pretty bad on Good Friday. The Savior of the world was dead. Could things get much worse? Just three short days later, everything had changed. I may feel my life is the worst it can be, but I give myself three days to pray and consider. Usually in three days things look different."

"I have learned a variety of friends is healthy for everyone's emotions."

"The best thing about growing up is that you are getting old enough to take control of a lot of things in your life, but your parents are still there to help you."

❀ ❀ ❀

Feelings are powerful. Have you ever said one of these things? "I don't feel good." "She hurt my feelings." "I'm not in the mood." "I'm lonely." Feelings are like thermometers telling us what's going on inside our hearts. In fact, the Bible says,

> *Happiness makes a person smile. But sadness breaks a person's spirit.*
>
> PROVERBS 15:13 ICB

Sometimes we think that our feelings have power on their own, that they're out of our control. We can't control what we're feeling all the time—but our feelings are connected to our minds and thoughts, our spirits or souls, and our bodies, too. By working with your mind and your body, you can change how you feel.

Your feelings are messengers, telling you what's going on inside. Don't ignore them or automatically obey them. Listen carefully, and with thought and prayer decide what to do next. Your thoughts are what you tell yourself about your feelings and anything else going on. Your actions are completely your choice.

You Asked

What are emotions, anyway? Like crying and stuff? Being happy?

Emotions are feelings—sometimes we refer to them as what's in our heart. Emotions include things like sadness, depression, anxiety, worry, fear, happiness, contentment, peace, and enjoyment. Emotions can be quick: "Stop that!" Or they can be moods: "I've been sad ever since I found out we're moving."

God created our complex bodies to work in a system. All parts work together—not independent of one another—like this:

Wonderfully Made

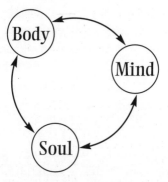

What you feel physically affects how you feel emotionally. If it's late at night and you're tired, hungry, or thirsty, you get upset more easily. You might feel hopeless or that a problem will never turn out right. Your body is giving you a signal through those feelings. That signal is *I need food, water, and sleep.* After a good meal or a good night's sleep the problem will still be there, but you may be able to clearly see how to solve it.

You might even wonder why it seemed like such a big deal the night before!

Our Mysterious Friends Return. . . .

Remember our friends the hormones? Not only are they running through our blood making physical changes, but they affect our emotions, too. It's not that they control how we act or feel, but they can make us more sensitive to certain emotions and situations. That can lead us to *react* rather than to *act* in planned ways as we would during the rest of the month.

For all women, from puberty on, our hormone levels are like ocean tides. They aren't at the same level throughout each month. Sometimes they're at low levels and sometimes at high levels. Just like tides, they usually come in predictable patterns. When our levels change, it can bring changes in our bodies that affect our moods.

- Estrogen is a hormone that your body begins to make more of as you progress toward being a woman. The right amount of estrogen may make us feel good about ourselves and happy with others.
- Progesterone is another female hormone. Sometimes progesterone can make us more likely to be sad or angry. It balances the estrogen, and it helps us to have a period, which is healthy for our bodies.
- Prolactin is a hormone, too. It will help you breastfeed if you have children someday. This hormone is also found in tears of emotion.

The hormone prolactin, which is higher in girls and women than in boys and men, chemically wires us to want to take care of children's needs. It's one reason you might like to baby-sit or work in the nursery!

These hormones gently cycle through their normal changes during the month and throughout your life. Most of the time they are even and balanced. Many young women don't feel these mood changes at all until a few days or a week before their periods. When their periods come, the month starts all over again, and their feelings are back to normal. Some girls don't feel mood shifts at all.

Charting your feelings on your calendar will help you understand how your emotions might change during the month. You can't direct the hormones, but knowing what they are and when they're coming will help you manage your actions. You really *do* have control.

January 2004

S	M	T	W	T	F	S
				1	2	3
4	5	6	7	8	9 *Sleepover!*	10 *ZZZ*☺
11	12	13	14 *PMS*	15 *PMS*	16	17
18 ☹	19 *P*	20 *X*	21 *X*	22 *E*	23	24
25	26	27	28	29	30 *Math test – STUDY!!!*	31

ZZZ = angry   ☹ = sad   P = period starts   E = period ends

I feel like crying a lot lately. How can I feel happy again?

Most feelings aren't necessarily related to hormonal changes; they're a normal part of everyone's life. Learning how to manage your emotions, to control your responses, and to think thoughts that affect how you feel is an important part of growing up.

Managing emotions is like navigating a boat. Rough waters come up, and you can see them. The waters are telling you something. Maybe you need to steer your boat elsewhere, or maybe you need to put up the sails and take advantage of the wind. Maybe you decide to hang on because it'll only be rough water for a few hours and then there's a smooth patch of beautiful blue ahead. Managing means you take in information and make calm decisions on how to act next. Even though your emotions are separate from others, how you handle them affects others. You can do things to help you figure out what you're feeling and what you should do next.

Looking Forward: Figuring Out Emotions

- Write in a notebook or journal. Don't worry about spelling or grammar or punctuation. Write down how you feel, what happened that led up to how you feel, and who was involved. Write down what was said and by whom. Write down anything that you think could help you feel balanced again. Balanced means content.
- Draw a picture showing how you feel inside.
- Do sports or any other kind of exercise. Exercise releases good substances, called endorphins, in your brain, reducing mood swings and helping you to think more clearly and calmly.
- Talk with someone you love and trust. A friend can help—if she works to help you see clearly rather than making you more upset. A parent is usually good.
- Pray. God always listens. He tells us to cast all of our cares upon Him, because He cares for us. He says that if we pray, with thanksgiving, He will give us peace.

*Don't worry about anything; instead, pray about
everything. Tell God what you need, and thank him for all
he has done. If you do this, you will experience God's
peace, which is far more wonderful than the human mind
can understand. His peace will guard your hearts and
minds as you live in Christ Jesus.*

PHILIPPIANS 4:6–7

This doesn't mean that we won't have trouble or concerns
or fear. In fact, Jesus tells us,

*"I have told you all this so that you may have peace in me.
Here on earth you will have many trials and sorrows. But
take heart, because I have overcome the world."*

JOHN 16:33

Though we will have problems, we won't be alone. God
provides comfort, helpers, answers, and peace. Once you've had
a chance to work through your feelings by writing, drawing,
exercising, talking, and praying, you're ready to take action.

If I think good things, will I stop feeling bad?

Our thoughts are what we tell ourselves. They result from
what we sense through our eyes, nose, ears, mouth, and touch
and how we make sense of what's around us. You might not
realize it, but you're talking to yourself all day. What you tell
yourself about any situation will affect how you feel.

Maybe your self-talk sounds like this: "I'm bad at this. I'm
going to get a bad grade. I hate school. Why do I have to be
here anyway?" What kind of feelings is that going to make?

What if you say instead, "I'll be okay. It's one test, and then
it's over. I studied well, and I know I can handle it. I can

always get help if I need to, and it's almost the weekend"? What kind of feelings is that going to make? Try it.

What you think and tell yourself about what is happening in your life really *does* change how you feel. Keep your self-talk positive to keep your mood feeling good.

Ask Your Dad

. . . what he does when he starts to feel bad about himself or about a job he's doing that isn't going well. How can you apply what he's learned, too?

Is it wrong to be mad? I always feel like I'm committing a sin if I'm mad at someone. It makes me totally uncomfortable, especially with my parents.

Anger is not a sin. The feeling is normal. God gets angry. Jesus got angry. Be honest with your emotions. If you're angry, say it: "I'm angry."

In this world, unfair things happen. Hurtful things happen. It would be silly and fake to pretend that these things don't make us mad. Anger is often a "secondary emotion." That means it follows after some other feeling that came first, even if it only came in a flash. Sometimes we get mad after someone hurts us or someone else, or when we're afraid or frustrated. Go back to when you first started feeling angry and think about what was happening at that time.

- Whom were you talking with?
- What had you just been talking about or thinking about?
- What were you trying to get done and couldn't?

While our emotions are messengers telling us how we feel—angry—the Bible is clear that we are responsible for our actions—the things we do and say in response to our anger.

Waiting a little while between when you're angry and when you act or speak is a choice you can make. The Bible says,

Don't sin by letting anger gain control over you. Think about it overnight and remain silent.

PSALM 4:4

It doesn't even have to be overnight, just enough time to cool off.

Okay, I'm still mad. Now what?

Decide among one of these things:

1) Am I really angry—or am I just tired, hungry, or stressed? Is it a little thing that is not likely to happen again? Is it something I can forget about—something that annoyed me rather than a big deal? Then let it go.
2) Am I just feeling sorry for myself? Am I being self-righteous or holding a grudge? Could this be my fault, too? Let it go or accept responsibility.
3) If you're still angry, talk with the person who made you mad. Keeping anger inside is like swallowing poison. If you eat food that's rotten or spoiled, your body reacts by making you sick so that you throw it up. Your body knows that keeping it inside will poison you. If you're mad at someone, you have to talk with that person or the anger will poison your feelings.

If another believer sins against you, go privately and point out the fault. If the other person listens and confesses it, you have won that person back.

MATTHEW 18:15

That's not easy. It's especially hard to tell your parents or good friends that you're angry with them, because you might be afraid it will damage the love between you or that it is disrespectful. In truth, honesty shows great love, especially when respectfully handled.

Pop Quiz

How should you talk with someone who has hurt you?

_____

_____

> *Be humble and gentle. Be patient with each other, making allowance for each other's faults because of your love.*
> EPHESIANS 4:2

Ask Your Mom

. . . to talk with you about something that made you mad this week. Figure out if you were feeling fear, frustration, hurt, or something else right before you got mad. You have to go back and take care of what caused that *first* feeling before your anger will go away.

> *But when you are praying, first forgive anyone you are holding a grudge against, so that your Father in heaven will forgive your sins, too.*
> MARK 11:25

All Christians have to forgive, and it's healthy for us inside and out. It may take a while to trust the person who hurt you, but you can forgive them—not hold a grudge anymore—right away.

Instead, be kind to each other, tenderhearted, forgiving one another, just as God through Christ has forgiven you.
EPHESIANS 4:32

Steps to Forgiveness

1) Clearly recognize the wrong done. What exactly was done or said?

2) With every wrong done, someone owes you something. This doesn't sound very "Christian," but it's true. If someone steals your computer, she owes you a new computer. What the offending person often "owes" you is an apology that includes admitting
   - what happened, and agreeing that it did happen;
   - that they did the wrong, and admitting it was wrong;
   - that it was against you and hurt you.

   They also owe you anything that can be repaired—like telling the other person they lied about you and setting the record straight. This might never happen, but the point is that you understand what is "owed" you.

3) Give the "debt list" to God to collect on. This frees you up to heal. It's also a very hard process because lots of doubts about God may arise, and it might take time. "Will God really make it right?" "Does God even care about what happened to me?" "Does forgiving mean it was okay?" "Does forgiving them mean I have to like them?" This takes time.

4) Mark your list of the debt(s) "Paid in Full," so the other person doesn't owe you anything now. You're out of the deal, and it's now between the other person and God only.

5) Treat the person who wronged you as forgiven. Don't remind her, hint about the wrong, or bring it up to other

people. It's done, over with, and in the past. Again, you may still not like her or even trust her. Forgiveness is NOT the same as rebuilding trust, liking somebody, or even making up with them. That is separate and may come after the forgiving process.

6) Accept the damage. This isn't accepting the blame, but it is taking action to do whatever you need to do to feel better and move on. Don't wait for somebody else to come along and rescue you and make it all better. You're the one who was wronged, so you speak up, ask for help, and move on. It's not always fair, but it's always right.

Ask Your Dad

. . . who the hardest person he's had to forgive was. How did he feel afterward?

Should I be happy most of the time?

Happiness and sadness often depend on our circumstances—what's going on in our lives and in our world. We're happy when we're going out to a movie or shopping or if a favorite grandparent is coming over. If we're hurt, bored, lonely, or afraid, we might feel sad.

Expecting to be happy all the time is going to lead to disappointment. Expecting to never be sad is going to lead to disappointment. Circumstances can't be perfect all the time. In between happiness and sadness is contentment—most of us can live with some moments of great happiness and some moments of great sadness. Learning to feel good with contentment—in the middle—is the secret to feeling good almost always.

That sounds good! What is contentment?

Contentment is being satisfied and pleased with what you have, not always needing more in order to feel good.

Pop Quiz

What makes me feel happy?

_____

_____

What makes me feel sad?

_____

_____

Am I a content person most of the time—or do I need more (more money, more beauty, more attention, more stuff, more fun, etc.) in order to be happy?

_____

_____

So it's wrong to be sad?

No. Sometimes sadness depends on what's going on in life. It's like getting a cold. You catch it, you feel crummy for a few days, and it goes away. Something may make you sad for a while, but then the sadness disappears.

Sometimes, though, the cold turns into something that hangs on and on. Then you need to go to a doctor and get it figured out. When sadness hangs on, you need to tell someone. Your body is telling you that something is happening in your heart, your mind, or your spirit that isn't healing.

Your life with God affects your emotions, too. Sin can make you feel sad or guilty. It's a way to let you know that something is wrong. Have you done or said something wrong and not asked God or another person to forgive you? If so, take care of that right away.

O Lord, you are so good, so ready to forgive, so full of unfailing love for all who ask your aid.

PSALM 86:5

People talk about depression like it's some kind of disease. What is it?

If your sadness is not because of something between you and God, and it's not a sadness that lifts right away with exercise, prayer, talk, or drawing, you might be depressed. Depression is not something permanent. You might think you'll never feel better again, but you will—I promise. Check the box next to each sentence below if it's something that's been happening to you.

- ☐ I've been feeling sad almost all the time for two weeks or more.
- ☐ I don't sleep well anymore—I have trouble falling asleep or wake up too early.
- ☐ I just can't deal with things in my life anymore.
- ☐ I want to eat to make myself feel better.
- ☐ I don't feel like eating at all anymore.
- ☐ I'm always tired.
- ☐ I want to be alone and away from family and friends a lot.
- ☐ Nothing sounds fun or interesting anymore—even things I used to enjoy.
- ☐ Things are never going to be right again.
- ☐ I have more thoughts about death, getting sick, or dying.
- ☐ I don't like myself anymore.

Talk with your parents or another trusted adult if you've been feeling any of these. Depression can often be healed by talking, counseling, or medication. You will feel better really soon.

You Asked

Sometimes I feel all jittery, like I have too much energy, only I can never burn it off. I can't get a song out of my head, and nothing makes me feel calm. My stomach aches, and I'm worried nothing is going to go right in my life. What's happening?

It sounds like stress. Kids get stress, too. Stress happens when we have too many things going on in life at the same time—too many expectations, commitments, things to do, places to be, people to please. Stress comes when we have little time to relax and have fun. Stress happens when we think we have to be perfect all of the time.

In fact, a life needs to be balanced. You need to make time for fun and rest. You need to expect yourself to fail at some things and make mistakes. Has there ever been a perfect person besides Jesus Christ? It's okay to be human and to grow. As Miss Frizzle of the *Magic School Bus* says, "Be messy! Make mistakes!" That's all part of a good life.

I'm worried!

Too much stress makes you feel anxious. Remember how the mind, the body, and the feelings all work together? When you're stressed, your body sends out hormones that can make your heart race and make you feel jittery. Those hormones can also make your stomach sick and make you feel like you'll never be calm.

Like many hormones, though, they come and go in waves. You can help yourself to relax, and those hormones will calm right down. A Japanese proverb says, "Calm the body, and the feelings will often follow." You'll be feeling like yourself again soon.

Try It

- Take a nap or read a book. Not a book for school but for fun.
- Exercise. Yep, back to those good brain substances again. Exercise releases them really fast.
- Talk with your parents or another trusted adult about the problems in your life. They can help you sort through and make changes that will allow you to be less stressed.
- Take a long warm bath with good-smelling bath salts. Warm baths release calming hormones. Never knew hormones were so important, did you?
- Expect yourself and others to make mistakes. It's okay. It happens, and it will all be passed over and out of your thoughts sooner than you think.
- Make changes in your life so you have time for fun, play, and rest.
- Don't expect perfection. Learn to say, "Oh well!" several times a day.

Ask Your Mom

. . . to give you a foot or ear massage next time you're stressed out. Rubbing your feet and ears has a wonderfully calming effect on your whole body. Try them both! You'll be surprised!

Pop Quiz

What does the Bible say is the most important emotion of all?

*If I didn't love others, I would be of no value whatsoever.
Love is patient and kind. Love is not jealous or boastful or
proud or rude. Love does not demand its own way. Love is
not irritable, and it keeps no record of when it has been
wronged. It is never glad about injustice but rejoices
whenever the truth wins out. Love never gives up, never
loses faith, is always hopeful, and endures through every
circumstance. . . . There are three things that will endure—
faith, hope, and love—and the greatest of these is love.*

1 CORINTHIANS 13:3B–7, 13

I Love You . . . I Think

Most people are easy to love most of the time—a good
friend, a parent, a brother, or a sister. Other times, it's hard to
feel love even for those closest to us. People make mistakes, or
they make us angry. They're human, too. Maybe a teacher
talked rudely to you or dismissed your idea. Maybe a friend
gossiped about you. Maybe your mom yelled or cut you off in
the middle of a sentence. It's not so easy to love then, is it?

As we grow up, we learn that there are different kinds of
love and that love is a decision we make, not only a feeling we
have. We can decide to act in love to a brother who is picking
on us or a friend who gossips about us. Loving those close to us
means gently sharing our feelings and then forgiving.

Sometimes the only way we can love someone is to ask God
to help us to do that. Pray and ask God to show you how to
love the person that you find unlovable at the moment.

Being loving doesn't mean you let everyone do or say anything to you at all times, though. Boundaries are important to
emotional health, too.

Am I in Love?

When we start growing up and noticing boys more, we
might start to feel warm feelings toward them when we haven't

felt those things before. Sometimes we just notice that boys aren't as bad as they used to be. Sometimes we think they're really cute. Because these feelings can be strong and are different from the feelings we feel toward our friends and family, we might think that's what being in love is. It's really called a crush.

What's a crush?

A crush is strong feelings of attraction and appreciation for a boy. Sometimes the feelings just swoop in—*whoosh*—and then a few days later they're gone, and you can't figure out what you thought was so great in the first place. Sometimes the feelings last longer. It's okay and normal to feel that some boys are nicer or cuter than other boys; all humans have preferences. It's smart to make a decision not to act on or talk about those feelings with boys instead of getting "carried away" by the moment. Your feelings will change as you grow. When you're older, you'll decide when to act on them and when not to. For now, just talk with your mom or a close friend about your feelings when they come up, and she can help you sort through them as well as keep your secret!

Looking Forward: Building Healthy Boundaries

Others do and say things that will affect you. Having boundaries means you learn to separate what's your problem or your fault from things that are *not* your problem or your fault. It's like sticking an invisible fence between your feelings and someone else's feelings. These fences are important to your health. You don't want to be a garbage disposer, taking in other people's problems, nor a garbage truck, dumping your problems on someone else.

Having boundaries means taking responsibility for your

own actions—but not for other peoples' actions or feelings. Each person is responsible for her own feelings.

If you blame your mother because you forgot your homework, you're moving into her boundaries. Your homework is your responsibility, not hers. If someone blames you for stealing her best friend, that is *not* your fault. No one steals another person—people choose their own friends. This time, that person is invading your boundary.

Learning not to blame but to problem-solve instead helps develop healthy boundaries.

Pop Quiz

(Think carefully before answering.)

Do you ever blame others for your mistakes?	Yes No
Do you feel responsible for making sure that your family is happy?	Yes No
Do you feel responsible for making sure that your friends are happy?	Yes No

We've learned about how our bodies, our minds, and our souls all cooperate. When we sin, we feel guilt and distance. That's one way our lives with God affect our feelings. But there's another wonderful way our relationship with God affects our feelings and well-being. The Bible says that the Holy Spirit is our helper. It also promises that when we let the Holy Spirit, God, control our lives, we will be like lovely trees with the loveliest fruit.

It doesn't mean we'll never have problems, never sin, or never need to learn. It does mean that, over time, God will produce that kind of fruit in our lives when we follow His ways through the choices we make and the actions we take—no matter what our feelings say at any given moment.

But when the Holy Spirit controls our lives, he will produce this kind of fruit in us: love, joy, peace, patience, kindness, goodness, faithfulness, gentleness, and self-control. Here there is no conflict with the law.

GALATIANS 5:22–23

Poetry

Dear Lord,
I love you and you love me.
I want to be the lady that you made me to be.
I don't want to be a sinner, just a winner
Who loves you.
    —by Chelsea, age 8

Loneliness is relative, the wise and learned may say,
For one is never alone, because our Lord will never
    stray.
But loneliness is a common place for those who live in
    strife.
I myself have been lonely; I have felt sad and without
    life.
Loneliness follows me in crowds and on my own.
Sometimes the loneliest place to me is when I'm not
    alone.
Sometimes my loneliness comes when the teasing will
    not end,
It always comes when I can't feel the Lord calling me
    His friend.
My Father above does care, and that is what I must see.
I must realize and accept my Lord's love for me.
For never will I feel so alone as my Savior did that day,
When He hung upon the cross for me and gave his life
    away.
He forgave my sins as he hung and died.
For all of his children he was crucified.
So that we may never feel lonely and stumble and fall,
Jesus was the loneliest of all.
So I'm not so alone with my Father so near,
When I call his name He will always hear.

So I will never be alone and without hope,
Because GOD will always help me to cope.
  —by Lynsey, age 14

Mom and Me
Ideas From Girls Like You

"We go on vacations together! I will also tell my mom I love her every day."

Kay and Dayna, age 10

"We plant flowers together in our garden—then when they bloom, we cut them and deliver bouquets to our neighbors."

Heidi and Chelsea, age 8

"When we're angry, we write down what we're feeling on a note pad and then talk about it when we're more calm."

Joann and Lynsey, age 14

Myself, My Family, My Friends

Growing up means . . . I know myself and others better—and we have more fun!

Girls like you say . . .

"I am nervous and excited at the same time about my feelings about boys as I grow up."

"What I like best about being my age is that I don't have to work a lot and I have lots of friends to be with."

"Don't forget that your mom and dad love you even though they drive you up the wall sometimes!"

"When I think about growing up, I think about living in a home with my own family."

71

❀ ❀ ❀

One of the most exciting things about growing up is that you get to meet new people, get closer with those you already love, and share more in your relationships. It's still fun to play with friends. But now friends are also for sharing secrets, for encouragement, and for trusting with important thoughts. Your mom might not only suggest what you wear—she might ask your opinion on *her* clothes, too. Your dad is interested in your plans and dreams and beliefs. Your brothers and sisters become your partners and sources of information and help. No matter who they're with, all of your relationships include one very important person—you! Jesus tells us . . .

Love your neighbor as you love yourself.
MATTHEW 22:39B ICB

That means, of course, that Jesus expects you to love yourself. Your relationship with yourself is very important, since it's where all the others start.

I have a relationship with myself? What's a relationship, anyway?

A relationship is how you *relate* to someone—how you talk with, what you do with, how you connect with, and how you care for someone, even if that someone is you! How do you treat people? Talk with people? What do you do with others? What do you share with others, trust to others, pray for others? All of those things are things you do for and with yourself. If you like yourself and treat yourself with respect, you're likely to be in healthy relationships.

Pop Quiz
Ten Things I Like About Myself

(Come on, fill them *all* in!)

1) My eyes

2) Hair color

3) Skin

4) height

5) Weight

6) Pimples

7) Smile

8) feet

9) hands (their soft.)

10) how I don't get moody while PMSing.

Sometimes the more we know about ourselves, the better we can like ourselves. We can see that although we're different from other people, we're special in our own God-planned way. Did you know that God doesn't compare you to anyone else? He loves you just as you are.

Who Am I?

A psychologist named Isabel Briggs Myers studied personalities and came up with four sets of choices that each person uses naturally, kind of like being left- or right-handed. Knowing which ways we like to do things helps us to better understand ourselves. Here are some definitions from her book *Introduction to Type.*

Where would you rather focus your attention?

"People who prefer **extraversion** tend to focus on the outer world of people and the external environment. You are energized by what goes on in the outer world. . . . Extraverts usually prefer to communicate more by talking than by writing. They need to experience the world in order to understand it, and thus tend to like action.

"People who prefer **introversion** focus more on their own inner world. Introverts tend to be more interested and comfortable when their work requires a good deal of their activity to take place quietly inside their heads. They like to understand the world before experiencing it, and so often think about what they are doing before acting."

How do you best find things out?

"One way to find things out is to use your . . . eyes, ears, and other senses (to) tell you what is actually happening, both inside and outside of yourself. **Sensing types** . . . become realistic and practical. They are good at remembering and working with a great number of facts.

"The other way to find out is through intuition, which shows you the meanings, relationships, and possibilities that go beyond the information from your senses. If you like intuition, you grow expert at seeing new possibilities and new ways of doing things. **Intuitive types** value imagination and inspirations."

How do you like to make decisions?

"One way to decide is through your thinking. When you use **thinking**, you . . . make decisions by analyzing and weighing the evidence, even including the unpleasant facts. People with a preference for thinking seek an objective (independent) standard of truth. They're frequently good at analyzing what is wrong with something.

"The other way to decide is through your feelings. **Feeling** considers what is important to you or to other people (without requiring that it be logical), and decides on the basis of person-centered values. Those with a preference for feeling like dealing with people and tend to become sympathetic, appreciative, and tactful."

How do you deal with the world?

"Those who take a **judging** attitude tend to live in a planned, orderly way, wanting to regulate life and control it. When you use your judging function, you like to make decisions, come to closure, and then carry on. (You) tend to want things settled.

"Those who prefer a **perceptive** process like to live in a flexible, spontaneous way. You gather information and keep your options open. (You) seek to understand life rather than control it, experiencing, enjoying, and trusting (your) ability to adapt to the moment."

Ask Your Mom and Dad

. . . what they think. Would they describe you the same way you describe yourself? How would your mom describe herself—and how would you describe her? How about Dad? Sometimes understanding how we operate helps us to love and appreciate ourselves. It can help us appreciate others, too, like our parents, our siblings, our best friends—and even people we don't like too much.

Take Care, Young Lady. . . .

Of yourself, that is. Taking care of yourself is an important part of loving yourself. Taking care of your body—eating well, sleeping, and developing healthy habits—is a good place to start. It means respecting yourself enough to be modest in what you wear—protecting yourself and refusing to draw unhealthy attention to your body. *The Inside-Out Beauty Book* talks more about modesty.

Also important is to take care of your emotional life—dealing righteously with emotions whenever they arise. As you grow older, make sure you choose healthy relationships. People in healthy relationships

- accept and love you for who you are, even if they encourage you to grow;
- respect your boundaries;
- value your skills, gifts, and talents as much as their own.

Try It

Write down the names of people close to you. Then ask yourself, "Does my relationship with them follow the three points above?"

Me: (Do I accept and love myself for who I am? Do I respect my own boundaries—not always trying to fix everyone else's problems? Do I value my skills, gifts, and talents, or am I jealous of others?) _____

Parents: _____

Brother: _____

Sister: _____

Best Friend: _____

Teacher: _____

Other: _____

You Asked

Speaking of parents, I heard that as kids get older they don't have a good relationship with their parents. I really like my mom and dad still. Does that have to change?

As you get older, your relationship with your parents will change. But you know what? It always has. They don't tie your shoes anymore, do they? They don't dress you in the morning. They're not putting you in a corner for a time-out, right? The way your parents relate to you has always changed as you've grown, and it will keep on doing that. The good news is, the more we grow together, the more we tend to love each other. So even as your relationship changes, your love can deepen, too.

The questions you'll have for your parents will change—as you get older, the questions get harder. But as you untie the ribbons that held you together as parent and little girl, you can be tightly tying the ribbons that hold you together as parents and young lady. The ribbons will change, but the love won't.

Yes, but my mom and dad seem to make me do the opposite thing of what everyone else is doing. Why is that?

Maybe your parents see that what the others are doing isn't healthy for you. Maybe they don't know your desires because you haven't spoken up. Maybe you haven't proved that you're ready for new responsibilities. One of the most important things that you can do with your parents is talk. Tell them what you'd like to do, and ask them what they think. If you ask respectfully, with honor, it's likely they'll answer with honor.

Growing up means you should be able to expect honest and reasonable answers from your parents, answers that take into account the fact that you're growing up. You deserve a relationship that treats you with respect. But parents must have the final say—they have the responsibility to raise you and will answer to God for the way that they do that. Growing up also means you begin to take more responsibility for yourself. And you must always treat your parents with honor—even when you're an adult. In the verse below, can you see the reward for doing that? Underline it.

Children, obey your parents because you belong to the Lord, for this is the right thing to do. "Honor your father and mother." This is the first of the Ten Commandments that ends with a promise. And this is the promise: If you honor your father and mother, "you will live a long life, full of blessing." And now a word to you fathers. Don't make your children angry by the way you treat them. Rather, bring them up with the discipline and instruction approved by the Lord.

EPHESIANS 6:1–4

Ask Your Mom

. . . to fill out this chart with you. Work together to figure out how you can smooth out the trouble spots.

Things I'm having trouble with:

(For example, *I don't like my chores, I wish I could stay up later, No one respects my ideas, I want to be able to go shopping alone with friends.*)

Problem: _____ Solution: _____

Problem: _____ Solution: _____

Problem: _____ Solution: _____

Problem: _____ Solution: _____

Things about me my parents are having trouble with:

(For example, *I have to be told many times to do something, I can be sassy, I don't pick up after myself.*)

Problem: _____ Solution: _____

Problem: _____ Solution: _____

Problem: _____ Solution: _____

Problem: _____ Solution: _____

This is how we learn from our parents and others in authority over us:

Watch me. . . . Do it with me. . . . I'll watch you do it.

The biggest way that your parents and others will believe that you are truly growing up, that you deserve more freedom and responsibilities, is by watching you. If you act, speak, and think in ways that tell people you deserve to be treated as a young adult, chances are it'll happen.

You are young, but do not let anyone treat you as if you were not important. Be an example to show the believers how they should live. Show them with your words, with the way you live, with your love, with your faith and with your pure life.

1 TIMOTHY 4:12 ICB

You Asked

Things aren't the same between me and my sister and brother anymore. What should I do?

Your relationship with your brothers and sisters will change as you grow, too. You probably don't fight over dolls or over who gets the cherry in the fruit cocktail anymore. Maybe now you fight over the telephone or what activities the family does. Friends will come and go, but your brothers and sisters will always be with you.

Siblings can annoy us, but they can also be a great source of information, encouragement, and friendship. One way to stay close as life changes is to find certain things you like to do or play together and then make sure you make time to do those things. If you don't have brothers or sisters, maybe a cousin or special family friend seems like one to you.

Try It

What do you like to do with your brothers or sisters?

_____

_____

_____

_____

Set aside at least one time each week to do these things with each of your brothers and sisters. Make sure you take responsibility to follow through.

Wonderfully Made

Did you know that women who live together, like sisters and even mothers and daughters, will often get their period at the same time each month? It's called synchronized menstrual cycles, and it's another way our bodies adjust to those around us.

Best Friends Forever

How many best friends have you had in the last three years? This year? Sometimes we have special friends who stick with us from year to year, and sometimes the Lord provides new friends for new seasons in life. Friendships change as we grow up, too.

I noticed. When I was younger, I had a lot of friends, and now as I am getting older, it's like everyone is narrowing down into these little groups. Is that okay?

As long as the groups are made up of people who want to be together and aren't mean it's okay. People naturally clump together with others who share the same interests. It's normal to want to hang out with people who think like you do. Also, friendships take time and trust, and there's not enough of that to share equally with everyone. So if you have a few special friends, that's okay. Just be careful not to be unkind or exclusive in choosing friends. If someone wants to join you and your best friend, don't be crabby because now there are three of you. Invite a fourth to join you three, and have even more fun. That way everyone has someone to be with.

Will my friendships become closer than ever as I grow up? Or will we grow apart?

Some will grow closer, and some will grow apart. Some friendships are based on circumstances—you're in the same class or go to the same church. If the circumstances change, the friendships might, too. Some friends will stick with you longer. Remember—there can be different levels and kinds of friendship. You might hang out with the kids in your neighborhood in the afternoon but only trust your deepest feelings to your best friend at church.

Remember that old saying, "Make new friends, but keep the old. Some are silver and the other gold." The truth is that sometimes the new friends turn out to be the gold. Keep your eyes and ears open in prayer to what people God is leading you to. He might be leading you to a great new best friend who will be faithful and loyal. Don't miss her because you're afraid to add new friends to your group.

I'm afraid that my friends and I won't do the right thing—that I'll be tempted to do wrong because they want me to, and then I'll do it.

Everyone is tempted to do things that are wrong—even adults. But everyone has tools for both avoiding and overcoming temptation. The best thing to do is to put yourself in situations where you are likely to be tempted less often. It's easier to say no ten times than to say it fifty times.

How can I avoid many tempting situations?

- Choose your closest friends from those who think like you and are committed to doing the right things.

You are not the same as those who do not believe. So do not join yourselves to them. Good and bad do not belong together. Light and darkness cannot share together.

2 Corinthians 6:14 icb

- Help and encourage one another to make good decisions.

Let us think about each other and help each other to show love and do good deeds.

Hebrews 10:24 icb

- Be aware of places and situations that will bring on temptations. Avoid them, and pray.

Keep alert and pray. Otherwise temptation will overpower you. For though the spirit is willing enough, the body is weak.

Mark 14:38

What should I do to overcome if I'm tempted to do wrong?

- Talk with people who will give you advice from the Bible.

Plans go wrong for lack of advice; many counselors bring success.

Proverbs 15:22

- Pray and ask God for a way out—then look for that way and take it.

But remember that the temptations that come into your life are no different from what others experience. And God is faithful. He will keep the temptation from becoming so strong that you can't stand up against it. When you are tempted, he will show you a way out so that you will not give in to it.

1 Corinthians 10:13

- Learn from the mistakes of others.

Dear friends, if a Christian is overcome by some sin, you who are godly should gently and humbly help that person back onto the right path. And be careful not to fall into the same temptation yourself.

GALATIANS 6:1

- Turn to God for help, and refuse to go along with wrong things.

So humble yourselves before God. Resist the Devil, and he will flee from you.

JAMES 4:7

Try It

Things I'm Sometimes   My Responses
Tempted to Do

_____   _____
_____   _____
_____   _____
_____   _____

Ask Yourself

Would I do this if my grandma was standing right beside me? My dad?

The goal is for you to be both physically mature and wise at the end of the growing-up road. Then you will be the person God wants you to be and the person those who love you see developing day by day.

So Jesus grew both in height and in wisdom, and he was loved by God and by all who knew him.

LUKE 2:52

Speaking of friends, is it normal to be thinking about boys?

Yes. Boys are people, too, right? As we grow, our interests grow, too. We are able to look beyond the few friends we've already had and see new and interesting things about other people. Some of those people are boys!

As hormones start leading us into adulthood, they will also make us look at boys with new eyes. God made us to appreciate one another. Just like any of your other friends, you will begin to see things in some boys that you appreciate and things in other boys that gross you out. There will be boys you like and admire and those you don't. It's okay to feel that one boy is nicer or more interesting than another.

Yeah, but is it okay to like boys? I mean, like talking about having one boy I like. My mom doesn't really think that it should be a big deal for me right now and that I should be friends with all the boys if I want to.

There are going to be boys that you like more than other boys, for a lot of different reasons. Some boys you'll have things in common with—sports you both like, a project you're working on together at school. You might admire how a boy works with others in your youth group or helps other people. Those are qualities you'd admire in any friend. Now that you're older, you're just noticing those qualities more in boys. That's a good thing. God has given men and boys wonderful characteristics, too.

Because God made men and women—and young men and young women—to appreciate one another, you'll also think there are certain boys that are cuter or nicer or more fun than other boys. That's okay, too. You're just deciding what you *like*, and therefore it's okay to like someone better than others, as long as you don't advertise those feelings.

At your age, though, your feelings are going to change all the time—remember? The boy you think is cute today might gross you out tomorrow. The boy you can't stand this year might turn out to be someone you like next year. Part of growing up is recognizing that we have changing feelings, because we're still figuring things out. It will save you lots of embarrassment if you don't declare your love for every boy you think is cute or nice—even just to the other girls. A little chat with your best friend or your mom is probably all that is required to share your feelings. There really isn't a reason to settle on one boy right now, because you will feel different every week, month, or year! The idea is to make many friends—both boys and girls—and enjoy their company together. Soon enough will come the time to focus on one boy only. If you don't spend time getting to know many different kinds of boys now, how will you even know what it is you like about young men? At the same time, you're allowing these boys to get to know you as a person—and that's what you want boys to appreciate about you. While everyone wants to look nice, nobody wants to be liked based only on looks.

Have fun! Enjoy each stage of your life without rushing too fast into the next one.

Looking Forward: Things Change

I'm afraid that . . .

- my grandparents are going to die.
- my dog is going to die.
- my friends won't remember me after I move.
- the kids at my new school won't accept me.
- my friends will leave me out when I homeschool.
- my brother will forget about me when he's in high school.

- things won't ever be right again after the divorce.

Change is life itself. Babies are born and grow up. You get older each day. You learn new things all the time. You know more people every year than you did the year before. These are all good changes—but they also require us to leave things behind.

When people or pets die, or when we move away from places we love, change schools, or have to start all over again with new friends, we grieve. That means we feel sorrow for what we have lost. Loss is a part of life; so is gain. We like to make new friends, have new pets, try new kinds of food, read new books, try new sports, buy new clothes!

Try It

Buy a photo-collage frame—one with many different openings for lots of pictures. Put some pictures in there of you when you were young, some old friends, some current friends, even people or pets who have now died or teachers from years past. Leave a few open spaces, too. Who do you think God will move into your life in the next few years? It will be exciting to see the pictures you will add.

In life we have to be prepared to say lots of hellos and lots of good-byes. A life without sorrow or grief is a life without love. Because it's only when we love that we feel sad when we lose something or someone. None of us wants to live without love, right? The good news is that there is one Person who will always be with you. Even though your relationship with Him will grow as you grow up, He never changes. He is always reliable, always loving, and always there.

Jesus Christ is the same yesterday,
today, and forever.
HEBREWS 13:8

Poetry

Mom and I

Mom and I are very close.
I always know that when I tell
Her a secret, it's safe with her.
We like a lot of the same things
Like scrapbooking and singing.
I love my Mom
And I know she loves me.
  —by Amy, age 11

I have some special friends, and they are very kind.
We all are a little different, but I don't think they mind.
Sometimes we have to say, "I'm sorry." And then wait for
  the reply,
And when they say, "I forgive you," you are so happy,
  you could fly.
We get together and do fun things;
That's what friendship brings.
We stick together through thick and thin and always
  have each other.
I think that might be because we listen to our mothers.
I hope my friendships last forever and always stay strong,
Because when I'm with a friend, I feel like I belong.
  —by Amy C, age 12

Mom and Me
Ideas From Girls Like You

"We have a weekend away—just the two of us."

"I just like talking with my mom. I always feel better after I
talk with her."

Bonita and Cara, age 10

"Go to the mall together—I can't wait till I can drive us there!"
Holly and Emmy, age 10

"I like baking things and helping Mom cook dinner sometimes."
Brenda and Amy, age 11

"Sometimes we go for ice cream and don't tell the boys. We snuggle on the couch when we watch TV together."
Joann and Lynsey, age 14

My Life With God

Growing up means . . .
I'm growing closer to the Lord—and it shows!

Girls like you say . . .

"Just when you think you have nowhere left to turn, when you feel your strength about to be spent, Jesus will come, and He will give you immeasurable love and support."

"When I think about growing up, I want to be a Christian with my family in a semi-large house in the woods or something."

"What I like best about my age is that . . . God has given me another year to live."

"What I like best about being my age is my church group and being older than the other kids at my school."

"When I was working in the nursery, I had a toddler fall asleep in my arms when even his mom couldn't calm him down. That was fun."

❀　❀　❀

We all want more control. We want to choose when and where to do our homework, what clothes we wear, how we spend our money. As you get older, you're getting more control. You get to choose what to do with your life!

With more control comes responsibility. We all make decisions based on our values. A Christian's decisions should be centered on her relationship with God. The important thing is to spend time with the One who will guide you. Then when a question comes up, He will guide you. When we spend time with and obey Jesus, we become more like Him inside, which makes the things we do and say more likely to be right. God is faithful to stick with us every day of our lives. He says He will never leave us nor give up on us.

> **Draw close to God, and God will draw close to you.**
> JAMES 4:8A

How do we draw close? Through all the things we do with and for Him—prayer, worship, giving, using our spiritual gifts for other Christians, obedience to His command to be baptized, remembering Him through Communion, and sharing Him with others are some examples.

For the law made nothing perfect, and now a better hope [Jesus] has taken its place. And that is how we draw near to God.

HEBREWS 7:19

You Asked

Great! How do I get started?

When you were little, your parents probably took care to teach you verses, to make sure you were reading a children's Bible, and to guide you toward God. They will still be there to guide you, but your mom and dad are in the process of transferring decisions to you. It's going to be your job to make sure that you're strong on the inside. And you're up to the job!

How can I be strong on the inside?

Think about it like a cell—which is shaped like a beach ball. Cells make up everything in your body. Only a thin layer keeps the insides of a cell inside it and the outsides outside it. It's important to have enough pressure from the inside of the cell so that when pressure comes from the outside the cell doesn't pop open. It doesn't want that outside stuff to force its way in and infect the inside.

You are like that cell. You're going to get pressure in this life—pressure to do wrong things, like cheat or steal or lie or be mean. Pressure to make bad choices to fit in. All of this is pressure from the outside. You need to have pressure from inside, too, to make sure you don't pop. What is that pressure? It's the good things you fill yourself up with—the Bible, praise songs, wisdom from godly people. Then when the pressure gets stronger on the outside, you're making it stronger on the inside, too, with the help of God, and your inside stays pure.

*For I can do everything with the help of Christ who gives
me the strength I need.*

PHILIPPIANS 4:13

Plug In

Your relationship with God is like turning on a lamp on a
dark day. You turn the lamp on in the morning, reminding
yourself of His love and care, and then you can see clearly to
do whatever you need to do for the rest of the day even if you
don't spend a lot of time after that thinking about the light. It's
just there, and you can make it brighter if you need to. You see
clearly to do your work, and you see clearly to have fun. It
doesn't have to take too long—just five or ten minutes—but
plug in the first thing in the morning by reading your Bible
and meeting with God in prayer.

*Tell me in the morning about your love. I trust you. Show
me what I should do because my prayers go up to you.*

PSALM 143:8 ICB

If you don't meet with Him in the morning, don't skip the
day. Plug in as soon as you can. Pick a place in the Bible and
begin reading through a book. Sing quietly, even in your head,
a line or two of a praise song you remember from church.
Then pray.

Sometimes I don't really know what to pray.

It can be hard to figure out what to pray. Sometimes people
follow simple outlines like PRAY: **P**raise, **R**epent, **A**sk, and
Yield. Sometimes it's easier just to remember to have a conver-
sation with God. You can do that any time of the day: "Help,
Lord!" or "What do I do now?" But you can also start and
close your days with these prayer lead-ins.

Try It

Hi, Jesus.
I think you are so _____.
It's amazing that you _____.
I'm glad that you _____.
Thanks for _____.
I'm sorry that I _____.
Please help me to _____.
Something is troubling me: _____.
Can you please help my friend (family, teacher, whomever)
_____?

Whatever you want me to do, Lord, let me know, and I'll do it.
   I think you want me to _____.
I love you.

You Asked

A lot of people in my church are talking about baptism. Do you have to be baptized to go to heaven?

The Bible says that God sent Jesus into the world to clean us from all the wrong things we have done. Because God is pure, He can't have a relationship with anyone who is not. We are not pure on our own, and we never can be, because we are not God. God sent Jesus to die for us and then be raised from the dead. His death paid the price for our bad choices. Only Jesus' death would do, because He is pure, too. That means it was a perfect sacrifice. This way, through Jesus, we are pure. Now we can have a relationship with God, who very much wants to be with us.

For God loved the world so much that he gave his only Son. God gave his Son so that whoever believes in him may not be lost, but have eternal life.

JOHN 3:16 ICB

We don't have to be baptized to get eternal life—life in heaven. Our faith is what gives us eternal life.

So why do people get baptized, then?

Baptism tells everyone about our relationship with God. We identify ourselves with Him—as part of His family. We're not hiding our faith.

The last instruction Jesus gave to His disciples as recorded in the book of Matthew is what we call the Great Commission, which means the job Jesus left for us to do. Jesus said,

> *"So go and make followers of all people in the world. Baptize them in the name of the Father and the Son and the Holy Spirit."*
>
> MATTHEW 28:19 ICB

We are to obey Jesus, baptize, and be baptized.

Some Christians baptize their babies as a way of identifying the babies with Jesus right away. They promise to raise the baby in a way that will lead the baby to know Jesus. Some Christians believe that baptism is something you do after you're old enough to understand and believe in who Jesus is and what He did on the cross for you.

Why do people go under water? Is it scary when everyone is watching you?

Baptism shows people on the *outside* that something has changed *inside* us, too. What's happening is we're showing that we have been "washed" by faith in Jesus so that we're pure before God now. It's a picture for everyone to see that we are now "clean." Baptism is a way of sharing with other Christians and the world that Jesus is our Lord and Savior and that He is alive in us!

When you were baptized, you were buried with Christ and you were raised up with Christ because of your faith in God's power. That power was shown when he raised Christ from the dead.

COLOSSIANS 2:12 ICB

Before we're baptized, we first show ourselves as the person we were born as. When we go under the water or have the water sprinkled over us, we show ourselves as burying that old self-dependent way. It's dead now. When we rise up after being baptized, we show that we have a new life—one that depends on God.

If you are older when you are baptized, it might seem scary if everyone is watching you or if you have to share a few words with people before your baptism. Don't worry about what other people are thinking. You are sharing love and encouragement with everyone who is watching. You are strengthening their faith in God, too. Jesus is present, loving and watching you, too.

Looking Forward

Have you been baptized? Would you like to be? Talk with your mom and dad about this.

What about Communion? What is it?

Communion is remembering Jesus' death until He comes back for us.

For every time you eat this bread and drink this cup, you are announcing the Lord's death until he comes again.

1 CORINTHIANS 11:26

Why do we want to remember and announce His death? It seems sad.

Actually, remembering Christ's sacrifice for us is a wonderful time because it reminds us of the life we have now and forever. Even after we become Christians, we are still human. We mess up and make mistakes or make bad decisions and act on them. This is called sin. Because God is pure, the penalty of sin is death.

Adam and Eve sinned against God. God told them that if they did that one particular sin they would die that very day.

But they didn't die right away, did they?

Yes and no. After they sinned, they did not die physically—in their bodies—right away, but spiritually they did. Their open relationship with God changed, and their inner persons were cut off from God. That is why all humans need a sacrifice in order to come clean before God, to be restored to Him now and forever. Everyone sins.

Adam and Eve were called in front of God and had to answer for what they did. They were really afraid, just like you are when you have to face your mom and dad after you mess up.

God loved them very much. God made a way that they could live in body and in spirit and by which His pure and holy law could still be kept. He took an animal, one that had done nothing wrong, and killed it in place of Adam and Eve. They had their sins paid for and the consequences covered by another—the innocent animal paid that price.

Do we kill animals anymore to take away our sin?

No. For a while God taught the people how to sacrifice an innocent animal in their place. The only problem was that each animal sacrifice only paid for the sins the people had already committed, and each year they would have to sacrifice again. How wonderful it would be to have all the penalty for our sins paid once and for all! God did this with Jesus Christ.

> *The next day John saw Jesus coming toward him and said, "Look! There is the Lamb of God who takes away the sin of the world!"*
>
> JOHN 1:29

When God came to earth and became a man, Jesus, he was the "lamb" that God provided. Only God is pure enough to completely pay the price for all our sins in the past and the future. When Jesus died on the cross, that one sacrifice made it possible for us to be clean again anytime we sinned from then on.

Who started Communion? Why do we eat bread or crackers and wine or grape juice?

When we celebrate Communion we obey Jesus, remembering Him and His gift of love when He died on the cross. Jesus started what we call Communion when He celebrated the Passover with his disciples. Passover is a special occasion that Jewish people still celebrate, remembering how God saved His people from being slaves in Egypt. Now God has saved us from being slaves to sin and from never-ending separation from Him.

> *On the night when Jesus was handed over to be killed, he took bread and gave thanks for it. Then he broke the bread and said, "This is my body; it is for you. Do this to remember me." In the same way, after they ate, Jesus took the cup. He said, "This cup shows the new agreement from God to his people. This new agreement begins with the*

*blood of my death. When you drink this, do it to
remember me."*

1 CORINTHIANS 11:23B–25 ICB

When we celebrate Communion, we remember God's
incredible love. Jesus loves you and is closer to you than even
your best friend can ever be.

Who can take Communion?

If you have unsolved anger or situations between you and
someone else, work it out before taking Communion. Communion is something to be taken seriously, with respect and
love. You might ask your Sunday school teacher or a pastor or
minister at your church about what the beliefs regarding Communion are at your place of worship.

Ask Your Mom and Dad

. . . about the first time they ever took Communion. What
did they think? What do they think about when they take it
now? Would they take Communion with you next time?

You Asked

What kinds of things can I do to help at church? Can kids do anything at all?

Yes, each Christian is given a spiritual gift when she
becomes a Christian. Kids too! The fun part is combining
something you like to do with the gift God has given you to
share with other Christians.

Pop Quiz
Find Your Spiritual Gifts

You can serve in many ways—kids are very important. Do you like to:

- ☒ Help younger kids learn verses or lessons? Do crafts with them in the nursery? Read stories to them? Baby-sit? *You might have the gift of teaching.*

- ☒ Give money to poor people or to the Salvation Army bucket at Christmas? Buy things for people who don't have much? Support a child in a poor country? *You might have the gift of giving.*

- ☐ Help people with their work? Clean up after Sunday school? Help your teacher in the classroom? Work behind the scenes to make things happen? *You might have the gift of serving.*

- ☒ Comfort people who are sad? Tell others how things worked out okay for you after a hard time? Bring food or gifts to people who need it? Make friends with lonely people? *You might have the gift of encouragement.*

- ☐ Make decisions to do the right thing even when it's hard? Share your opinion with others if you feel it can help them, too? Come up with ideas that everyone can do with you to help at home, school, or church? *You might have the gift of leadership.*

- ☒ Find something good in everyone you see? Write notes or draw pictures for people who need some thoughtfulness? Make sure everyone gets invited or involved? *You might have the gift of kindness.*

All of these are things kids can do.

Here are some places in the Bible where you can read about spiritual gifts:

Romans 12:4–8
1 Corinthians 12:4–12
2 Timothy 1:6
1 Peter 4:10–11

Being a part of the Christian body also means that you do things with the rest of the body. You haven't seen any feet walking around without legs and hips, have you?

When we have a lot to do, it can be hard to make sure we give church a priority. The Bible says,

> *Let us think about each other and help each other to show love and do good deeds. You should not stay away from the church meetings, as some are doing. But you should meet together and encourage each other.*
> HEBREWS 10:24–25A ICB

So should all of my friends be Christians?

Your *best* friends should be Christians.

Joining with someone is a way of having an extra-close relationship—like a best friend. You will have many friends, though, and not all of them will be Christians. In fact, that's how a lot of people become Christians. Studies show that most people who become Christians do so before they are adults—while they are still kids! A friend can show others how different—peaceful, wonderful, and important—life can be with Jesus in control.

Talk Their Talk

Be sure to use language your non-Christians friends can understand when you talk to them. Sometimes Christians get so used to using "church language" or "Christianese" that they forget others might not understand what they mean!

Christianese	Translation
Scripture or Bible verse	a place in the Bible where it says . . .
believe	trust, accept
converted	changed, transformed
Christian	follower of Christ
confess	admit
find the Lord, get saved	accept Christ, make a decision to follow Christ, give control of your life to Him
grace	God's totally unearned forgiveness
Gospel	God loves us and sent His Son so that we can find forgiveness and new life through Him
have a burden	be concerned
know	believe, trust, be certain, be sure
the Lord	God, Creator, Jesus
the Holy Spirit	God the Spirit, the Spirit of God
praise	thanking God for His greatness
pray	talk with God, ask God
preach	talk about, teach
repent	to be sorry about wrongs, admit your responsibility, and turn from them
salvation, saved	forgiven of wrongs and given eternal life
Savior	Jesus, God's Son, who forgave my wrongs and gave me eternal life

share	discuss, explain
sin, sinner	acting against God's will and offending God's character
testimony	story of how you became a Christian and what God is doing in your life right now
witness	tell about, show others
worship	giving honor and glory to God

Remember, God wants to be close to you, teach you, laugh with you, and share secrets. He'll help you make good choices as you gain more control of your life. Jesus wants to be your Best Friend Forever. Will you ask Him to be?

The greatest love a person can show is to die for his friends.
JOHN 15:13 ICB

Looking Forward:
My Life Joined With Christ's

Today's Date:
Dear Jesus,
    I want to follow you. I understand that I have made wrong choices in my life. I have tried to do things my way instead of your way. I'm sorry. Please forgive me for those decisions, and help me to make good choices from now on. I understand that I have control in my life. I freely give that control to you. I will follow you from now on.
    Thank you for dying on the cross so my sins can be completely forgiven and for rising from the dead to live

again. I know that you love me. I want to love you, too.
Please teach me how.

Love,

_____

Whom will you tell about this decision? _____

When? _____

Poetry

God, please help me as I grow up to serve you with all
    my heart.
Please give me opportunities to help others.
Please help me to trust you more.
God, I am a little scared about growing up.
Please stay with me and guide me through life.
God, I love you and my family so much.
    —by Amy, age 12

Sugary, sweet, salty, sour . . . God has the most power.
    —by Dayna, age 12

Lord, guide me as I grow
And show me where to go.
Help me remember to pray
And teach me new things every day.
Show me how to love
And thank you for watching over me from above.
    —by Emmy, age 10

Mom and Me
Ideas From Girls Like You

"We love mother-daughter devotions together."
    Debbie and Sarah, age 10

"We love to sing praise songs in the car—and make up our
own verses to go with them. Sometimes we write our own
praise songs on the piano."
    Sandra and Elizabeth, age 8

"One of my favorite pages in my scrapbook is from when I got
baptized at the beach. It was sunset and the pictures turned out

really good, so we put together some very special pages that show just how it happened. I can look back and always remember my promise and God's."

Robin and Rachel, age 15

School and Activities

Growing up means . . .
I'm working hard and learning what I like!

Girls like you say . . .

"When I'm doing homework, sometimes it feels like it's taking forever to finish. But in reality it's only been a few minutes!"

"What I like best about being my age is . . . I win the games in PE."

"It's going to be fun when I can go to college. I want to study swimming."

"I can't wait to be a teacher."

※ ※ ※

One of the best things about growing up is looking for-
ward toward the future. As you get older, what you like
and are good at becomes clear. You're also more sure about
what you don't like so much or what you have to work harder
at. It's great to know what you do well and the talents you can
share with others. It makes you more confident!

Learning is a big part of our lives—whether you homeschool, go to public school, or go to Christian school. When
you add other activities to that, like arts and sports, you
become a well-rounded young woman who knows what she
likes and who has learned to enjoy life. You don't just snap into
adulthood at eighteen—you're already becoming the woman
you are to be. What kind of woman do you want to be? Well-
read and knowledgeable? Skillful? Wise? Understanding? Fun?
Hooray! These are all great areas to develop in your life.

Take time to do all of your work well, because it shows
what kind of a person you are on the inside. Sometimes it can
be hard to do work you don't enjoy and not want to rush
toward the activities you *do* enjoy. In the end, though, you'll
get to spend more of your time doing what you enjoy but will
be well-educated and able to enjoy many aspects of life.

Work hard and cheerfully at whatever you do, as though you were working for the Lord rather than for people.
COLOSSIANS 3:23

You Asked

I tried hard, but I got a C.

When you do your work, God looks at the effort you put into it, not the results. He looks at a person's heart. If you work hard and do your best, you are probably still going to end up with some A grades, some B grades, some C grades, and perhaps even lower from time to time.

People judge by outward appearance, but the Lord looks at a person's thoughts and intentions.
1 SAMUEL 16:7B

Grades aren't judges of you as a person. They just tell you about how you are interacting with your work. When you get a high grade, it normally means you're doing well with work that isn't too hard for you and that you enjoy to some degree or another. Average grades are just what they say—they're typical. It means you're doing good work, and that's okay. Lower grades indicate that you either don't understand, aren't applying yourself, or are working in an area you don't like or aren't suited for. You might need help, and that's okay, too.

We all have to do work that we don't like in order to meet requirements. Even if you love English, you have to know math to get along in the world. So do your math (or reading or whatever it is that's hard for you) to the best of your ability.

Then spend your free time or elective courses doing what you love.

Get all the advice and instruction you can, and be wise the rest of your life.

PROVERBS 19:20

Did You Know?

People can be "smart" in many different ways. In fact, we each have areas that we are smart in, though they may not look like the ways your friend is smart. That's the beauty of it— we're each different and gifted in our own blend of ways. A man named Howard Gardener first thought about and explained the seven different ways to demonstrate intellectual abilities. One woman, Liz Bogod, put together the information like this:

Pop Quiz

Do you like to . . .

☒ look at maps, charts, pictures, videos, and movies? Then you might have a high **visual/spatial intelligence**. You're probably good at
- puzzle building
- reading and writing
- sketching and painting
- constructing, fixing, and designing practical things

Some activities you might enjoy that could lead to a future career could include navigating, sculpting, photography, inventing, architecture, interior design, mechanics, or engineering.

SANDRA BYRD

☐ listen and talk and think in word pictures? You might have a high **verbal/linguistic intelligence**. You're probably good at
- speaking, writing, storytelling
- explaining, teaching
- using humor
- convincing others to your point of view

Some activities you might enjoy that could lead to a future career could include poetry, journalism, writing, teaching, law, politics, translating.

☐ use reason, logic, and numbers? You might have a high **logical/mathematical intelligence**. You're probably good at
- problem solving, classifying, and categorizing information
- questioning and wondering about natural events
- doing controlled experiments

Some activities you might enjoy that could lead to a future career could include science, designing, making up computer programs or Web sites, doing research, accounting, and working with money.

☑ express yourself through movement? You might have a high level of **bodily/kinesthetic intelligence**. You're probably good at
- eye-hand coordination
- sports
- crafts

Some activities you might enjoy that could lead to a future career could include dancing, sports, crafts, acting, miming, mechanics, sewing, PE teacher.

appreciate and produce music? You may have a high level of **musical/rhythmic intelligence**. You're probably good at

- singing
- playing musical instruments
- remembering melodies and songs

    Some activities you might enjoy that could lead to a future career could include music, disc jockeying, singing, composing.

relate to and understand others? You may have a high level of **interpersonal intelligence,** which means you see clearly how others might feel and act. You're probably good at

- seeing things from other people's point of view in order to understand how they think and feel
- organizing
- maintaining peace in group settings and encouraging cooperation

    Some activities you might enjoy that could lead to a future career could include peer counseling, sales, teaching.

think about how you're feeling, and be aware of what's happening inside you? You may have a high level of **intrapersonal intelligence**, which means you see clearly *within* yourself. You're probably good at

- seeing your own strengths and weaknesses
- reasoning with yourself
- understanding your role in relationship to others

    Some activities you might enjoy that could lead to a future career could include research, studying theory, or philosophy.

Wonderfully Made

I, ___Olivia___, am wonderfully made. I am smart, though my kind of intelligence may be different from that of those around me. In fact, I think that my best intelligences, chosen from the list above, are _musical/rhythmic_ and _intrapersonal intelligence_, I can't wait to see how God uses them in my life and others' lives!

Did You Know?

There are different ways to learn, take in information, and remember it. Once you find out which ways you learn best, you can help yourself to find those ways and learn/remember even better!

Visual learners learn through seeing things. They like to see the teacher, take notes, and look at diagrams and textbooks.

Auditory learners learn through hearing. They like to listen to lectures, have discussions, and listen to books on tape.

Tactile learners learn through doing. They like to learn through a hands-on approach, feeling things, being involved. They sometimes find it hard to sit still for long periods of time.

Ask Your Mom and Dad

. . . what kind of learning style they have. What kind of learning style do they think you have?

The Choices Get Harder

A lot of times we need to make decisions on what to get involved with, because any sports and activities you get involved with require time and money. You'll want to spend both wisely. Knowing what you like and what you're good at can help you make good decisions. Knowing that decisions have consequences can help you to think carefully before you make them. So can having a simple decision-making process—like this one, developed by Six Seconds at their site *www.6seconds.org.*

Making Decisions

1) **Choose.** Consider what you want—what results will you call a success? Recognize these things:
   - I have a choice.
   - There are many options, and some will work better than others.
   - My choice might get me the results I want.

2) **Do.** Now you need to try what you've said you want to try.
   - If I choose to do nothing, that is still a choice.
   - I'm going to take the power and responsibility for the choices I make.

3) **Evaluate.** Did I get what I wanted? What else did I get? Use this information to make good choices next time.

Did You Know?

The word *choice* not only means a decision to be made between two things, it also means "the very finest." Make sure all of your choices are *choice*!

The whole future stretches in front of you. Your Lord knows all of your ways and all of your days. Your life is a gift from Him. Enjoy the way He made you and all of the things He made you to enjoy to do!

You saw me before I was born. Every day of my life was recorded in your book. Every moment was laid out before a single day had passed. How precious are your thoughts about me, O God! They are innumerable!

PSALM 139:16–17

Poetry

School

My school is a public school where the kids work and
   play.
The teachers are good—like they should be.
We learn each and every sun-rising, rain-filling,
Cold-nipping, sun-dripping day.
It is hard, sweat-cracking work but . . .
The day has an end and I go through the forest on the
   big yellow bus
And have a fun-filling, joy-bringing family evening.
   —by Elizabeth, age 8

Homeschool

A long day of sun and rain,
Homeschool is exciting, not all that plain.
A long day of writing and reading,
At least I am succeeding.
A long day full of fun and games,
Reading by the fireplace and watching the flames.
A long day with my pets and family,
Doing devotions together happily.
   —by Stephanie, age 12

Mom and Me
Ideas From Girls Like You

"My mom is teaching me how to sew. Someday we'll sew my
wedding dress—together!"

Kelly and Katy, age 11

"We love to go to horse expos together—just the two of us."

Doreen and Casey, age 10

"Crafts! Designing scrapbooks and scrapbooking together."

Linda and Maile, age 9

"When I left Queen's my future seemed to stretch out before me like a straight road. I thought I could see along it for many a milestone. Now there is a bend in it. I don't know what lies around the bend, but I'm going to believe that the best does. . . ."

Anne's horizons had closed in since the night she had sat there after coming home from Queen's; but if the path set before her feet was to be narrow she knew that flowers of quiet happiness would bloom along it. The joys of sincere work and worthy aspiration and congenial friendship were to be hers; nothing could rob her of her birthright of fancy or her ideal world of dreams. And there was always the bend in the road!

" 'God's in his heaven, all's right with the world,' " whispered Anne softly.

from *Anne of Green Gables*
by L. M. Montgomery

Last year I bought a pair of jeans for my daughter that I knew were too big for her. I loved them, though, and so did she. They were the perfect cut and style for her and had a groovy design on the cuff. We stuck them into the back of her drawer, knowing she would grow into them.

She did. Recently she pulled them out and put them on. They zipped right up and looked as nice as we'd hoped they would. Growing up is great.

Live with honest love and grace for yourself and others and accept and embrace the life you've been given with an open mind and open heart. Grow into that great future that has been waiting expectantly in the back of the drawer for you to be just the right size. Become the lovely young lady the Lord means for you to be.

And now, dear reader, my blessing for you:

I pray that your hearts will be flooded with light so that you can understand the wonderful future he has promised to those he called.
EPHESIANS 1:18A

Acknowledgments

Many thanks to the people who kindly allowed me to use, rephrase, or otherwise utilize their thoughts and materials for the benefit of this book.

Opening and Closing

- *Caddie Woodlawn,* reprinted here with the permission of the heirs of Carol Ryrie Brink.
- *Anne of Green Gables,* reprinted here with the permission of the heirs of L. M. Montgomery. *L. M. Montgomery* is a trademark of Heirs of L. M. Montgomery Inc. *Anne of Green Gables* and other indicia of "Anne" are trademarks and Canadian official marks of the Anne of Green Gables Licensing Authority Inc.

Section One

- Information on tobacco use from the Surgeon General's report as listed at *www.cdc.gov/tobacco/sgr/sgr4kids /realdeal.htm.*
- Portion sizes courtesy of Dr. Christine Wood of *www.kidseatgreat.com.*
- BMI Growth Charts came from *www.cdc.gov/growthcharts.*

Section Two

- Steps to Forgiveness and garbage illustrations courtesy of Tim Sanford.

Section Three

- MBTI information courtesy of Consulting Psychologists Press, taken from the book *Introduction to Type* by Isabel Briggs Myers. 3803 East Bayshore Road, Palo Alto, CA 10096. *www.cpp-db.com.*

Section Four

- Christianese chart courtesy of *www.Spirit1053.com.*

Section Five

- Paraphrase of Multiple Intelligence information and learning styles information used by permission of Liz Bogod *www.ldpride.net/learningstyles.MI.htm.*
- Decision-making chart used with permission of *www.6seconds.org.*

For professional review and contributions, thanks to

- Gia Hemmen, M.D., a family practitioner specializing in women's and children's medicine.
- Tim Sanford, a licensed professional counselor with over twenty years' experience working with teens, and the author of *I Have to Be Perfect.*
- Michael Byrd, M.Div., reviewer of all biblical materials.
- Brenda Abelein, Debbie Austin, and Robin Gunn, moms extraordinaire.

Mother-Daughter quote, idea, and poetry contributors:

Brenda and Amy Abelein
Debbie and Sarah Auston
Doreen and Casey Button
Elizabeth Byrd
Stephanie Conrod
Bonita, Amy, and Cara Crumley
Joann and Lynsey Harrison
Heidi and Chelsea Holmlund

Kaylynn and Emily Mills
Linda and Maile Miyake
Deb and Tavia Raney
Bev and Tori Whipple
Kay and Dayna Wiesmann
Kelly and Katy Wilkerson
Holly and Emmy Yacapin

All efforts were made to locate the original source of any permitted materials. Please contact author, below, with any questions and/or comments.

Sandra Byrd
P.O. Box 1207
Maple Valley, WA 98038

Answering Questions From
Girls Just Like You!

Sandra Byrd loves interacting with girls like you who read her books. In fact, she gets letters all the time and has developed a series of books that address the questions asked to her most often.

In *Girl Talk* Sandra covers issues from school, family, friends, and more including:

- Why do I look different all of a sudden?
- Could terrorists really blow up my school?
- Do you think parents love some children more than others?
- How do you know the Bible is real?

In *The Inside-Out Beauty Book* she looks at health, beauty, and how to not lose focus on staying beautiful *inside*. Topics she addresses include:

- Who am I?
- How should I act?
- How should I dress?
- What should I do about makeup?

Join the fun and see what girls just like you across the country are talking about!